A CHANCE TO MAKE HISTORY

What Works and What Doesn't in Providing an Excellent Education for All

WENDY KOPP

Founder of
TEACH FOR AMERICA

with STEVEN FARR

Praise for Wendy Kopp's *A Chance to Make History*

"Over the last two decades, Teach For America has become an engine for bringing talent to struggling public schools, and in the process, generated a force for reform. Wendy Kopp's recent book, *A Chance to Make History*, makes that case powerfully." — *Huffington Post*

"An optimistic narrative about school reform from an author with an unusual perspective. . . . Kopp's insistence on aiming high should make it required reading for all professional educators." — *Kirkus Reviews*

"Kopp's new book written with Steven Farr, *A Chance to Make History: What Works and What Doesn't in Providing an Excellent Education for All*, offers an intriguing summary and analysis of all she has wrought. . . . Kopp's book makes many valid if counter-intuitive points about why Teach For America makes sense." — *Washington Post*

"Kopp offers a perspective on lessons learned as she spotlights particularly effective teachers and techniques that have helped poor children from under-performing schools to exceed standards and get into college. Following pro-files of teachers and schools, she offers lessons that are widely applicable." — *More magazine*

"How can we scale up the success of great teachers who have demonstrated again and again that poor children can learn and succeed in school? This is the essential question Wendy Kopp addresses in *A Chance to Make History*. Ac-knowledging that there are no easy answers or 'silver bullets,' Kopp calls on us to move beyond ideological differences and territorial disputes and come together to transform American education."
— **Marian Wright Edelman, president, Children's Defense Fund**

"Sure to inspire both current and future teachers." — *Library Journal*

"The strength of *A Chance to Make History* is in documenting that genuine reform can and is taking place throughout the country." — *Education Next*

"America's history is a story of struggling to fulfill fundamental ideals of free-dom, equality, and opportunity. Today the frontier of that struggle is in our schools, and amid all the debate about education reform, this book is exactly what we need. Wendy Kopp draws on the collective wisdom of the thousands of brilliant teachers who have gone through the program she founded. They have become deeply informed agents for transformational change. By reading this book, you can become one as well."
— **Walter Isaacson, author, historian, and president and CEO of The Aspen Institute**

A **CHANCE**
TO MAKE **HISTORY**

What Works and What Doesn't

in Providing an Excellent Education for All

WENDY KOPP

Founder of TEACH FOR AMERICA

With **STEVEN FARR**

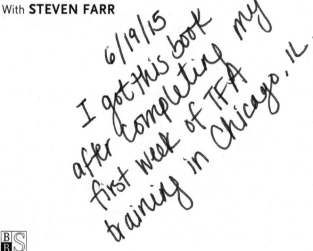

6/19/15
I got this book
after completing my
first week of TFA
training in Chicago, IL.

PUBLICAFFAIRS
New York

Type set in Stemple Garamond

The Library of Congress has cataloged the hardcover as follows:

Kopp, Wendy.
    A chance to make history : what works and what doesn't in providing an
excellent education for all / Wendy Kopp with Steven Farr.—1st ed.
       p.   cm.
    Includes bibliographical references.
    ISBN 978-1-58648-740-9 (hardcover : alk. paper)
    ISBN 978-1-58648-926-7 (e-book)
    1. Effective teaching—United States. 2. Academic achievement—United
States. 3. Teach for America (Project)—History. I. Farr, Steven. II. Title.
LB1025.3.K667 2011
371.1020973—dc22

                                                                        2010036774

Paperback ISBN: 978-1-61039-104-7

10 9 8 7 6

CONTENTS

AUTHOR'S NOTE TO THE PAPERBACK EDITION

Since *A Chance to Make History*'s hardcover publication in January 2011, public discussion around the core ideas it explores has become all the more vibrant. Evidence of the transformational potential of education for children in low-income communities is growing, as school systems like New Orleans continue to raise student performance levels. In districts and states across the country, new leaders are on a mission to dramatically improve outcomes across entire school systems. Among these leaders are several Teach For America alumni—including Cami Anderson as superintendent in Newark, Kaya Henderson as chancellor in D.C., John White as superintendent in New Orleans, Kevin Huffman as Tennessee's state commissioner of education, Chris Barbic as superintendent of Tennessee's most struggling schools, and Vanessa Rodriguez as superintendent of the New York City district that serves students in alternative education programs (including youth in the criminal justice system).

Political leaders and advocates, including students' families and active teachers, have worked together to effect state-level policy changes grounded in the insights drawn from schools and school systems that are effecting meaningful student progress. While there are many factors fueling these changes, chief among them is a growing critical mass of teachers who are proving the transformational power of education at the classroom level each and every day.

In February 2011, nearly 11,000 Teach For America alumni, corps members, and supporters convened in Washington, D.C., to consider both the extraordinary progress made over the past two decades and just how far we still need to go to realize our vision. The energy in the conference hall was palpable. As Geoffrey Canada, the visionary and determined founder and leader of the Harlem Children's Zone, reflected, "I never thought I would see this moment. I thought we would go down fighting for the cause. . . . But now I'm thinking we could really win!"

As the thousands and thousands of teachers, school leaders, elected officials, community organizers, advocates, and leaders left that summit, one question rang in our ears: What role will I play?

My hope is that this book will raise that question anew, and that each of us will decide to step up and lead our movement forward on behalf of millions of children who have the potential to make history.

WENDY KOPP
November 2011

INTRODUCTION

W HEN I FIRST DREAMED up the idea of Teach For America, I envisioned our generation rallying to address the unjust reality that even in our nation—a nation that aspires so admirably to be a place of equal opportunity—the neighborhood into which children are born still largely predicts their educational outcomes and, in turn, opportunities in life.

In the year of the twentieth anniversary of our launch, 46,000 graduating seniors, recent college graduates, and young professionals, of all academic disciplines and career interests, applied to Teach For America, revealing that the opportunity to address this injustice is more inspiring than ever. More than 5 percent of the senior classes at more than 130 public and private institutions, including 20 percent of the seniors at Spelman College and 15 percent of the seniors at Princeton University—where I first proposed the creation of a national

1

teacher corps in my undergraduate senior thesis in 1989—competed to teach in our nation's most underresourced communities.

Two decades into Teach For America's history, more than 8,000 corps members are teaching across thirty-nine cities and rural regions. They are throwing themselves into their work, going above and beyond traditional expectations to expand the opportunities available to their students. Rigorous research shows they are having a positive impact in the highest-need classrooms in the country.[1]

At the same time, more than 20,000 alumni have completed their two-year commitments. Twenty years in, we are seeing confirmation of Teach For America's initial proposition—that corps members' teaching experience would not only have a positive impact on students but also influence the priorities and long-term decision making of the corps members themselves and ultimately create a leadership force for long-term change. Although few of our alumni had originally intended to enter teaching at all, more than 60 percent are still working within the field of education today, and many others are working to impact schools and low-income communities from other fields. The ranks of alumni include hundreds of award-winning teachers, successful urban and rural school principals, school district leaders, social entrepreneurs, teacher educators, policy makers, and engaged citizens working to improve education, as well as lawyers, doctors, and nonprofit executives working to take some of the pressure off urban and rural schools by improving the conditions of low-income communities.

I have been inspired and humbled by the extraordinary commitment of our corps members and alumni. More important, I have learned from them—and from our colleagues in communities across the country—that although the obstacles are considerable, it is possible to actually solve this problem of educational inequity. It has always been possible for a tiny fraction of children growing up in low-income areas to beat the odds and find a path to achieving the American dream. But what I have seen over the past twenty years is hard evidence that we can ensure all of our children in urban and rural communities have the opportunity to attain an excellent education.

This book is an effort to share what our corps members, alumni, and colleagues have taught me about the problem of educational inequity and what it will take to solve it.

A NATIONAL INJUSTICE

On the Upper West Side of Manhattan, where my husband Richard and I are raising our family, our three school-age boys attend public schools. Chances are good that they will read and write and do math at grade level, even without heavy lifting on our part or extraordinary motivation and ability on their part. I say all this with trepidation as I'm a nervous parent, my kids are still young, and of course I wonder some days whether they will make it at all. The default and likely path, however, is that unless they fall far below the averages, they will finish high school and college and end up with an array of professional options.

A few blocks north, the statistical odds of success are very different. Unless parents or their children demonstrate extraordinary and sustained effort while juggling all the challenges of poverty, and get some lucky breaks as well in the form of access to special opportunities and extra supports and resources, the statistically probable path is that a child will not attend college and will not enjoy the breadth of educational, economic, and life opportunities that my children will likely enjoy. This is due not to differences in ability or motivation but rather to the luck of their birth.

Children in low-income communities are, on average, two to three years behind in reading skills by the time they reach fourth grade.[2] Half of them will not graduate from high school.[3] Those who do graduate will read and do math, on average, at the level of eighth graders in high-income areas.[4] These gaps impact African American, Latino, and Native American students most severely because they are much more likely than Caucasian students to face the challenges of poverty.

The consequences of these disparities are devastating for the more than 15 million children in our nation who are growing up below the poverty line, for their families, and for our society. High school dropouts have three times the unemployment rate of college graduates.[5] Young male high school dropouts are a shocking forty-seven times more likely than college graduates to be incarcerated.[6] Given the dramatically disproportionate representation of children of color in schools in underresourced communities, this problem is a serious obstacle to racial equity—decreasing the diversity of our college campuses, workplaces, and the ranks of political and economic leadership. The problem also weakens our economy; a recent study shows the economic impact of the achievement gap to be hundreds of billions of dollars—contributing to the "economic equivalent of a permanent national recession."[7] And needless to say, we will not fulfill the potential of a strong democracy if whole generations of children in the historically most disenfranchised communities don't have the basic skills and critical thinking skills to engage fully and make good decisions. When we fail to ensure our children attain a quality education, we pay a massive cost—in moral, civic, and economic terms.

NEW OPTIMISM IN THE FACE OF A PERSISTENT PROBLEM

Our policy makers and educators have been grappling with this challenge for decades. In the sixties and seventies, we committed to desegregate schools in order to ensure that all of our nation's students have access to an equal education. Unfortunately, though, poor and minority students continued to lag academically. Sociologist James S. Coleman exposed this reality in 1966 in the widely cited "Coleman Report," which showed that—given the weak influence of schools at the time—students' background explained 90 percent of their achievement in school.[8]

Twenty years ago, the prevailing assumption in most policy circles was that socioeconomic circumstances determined educational outcomes. We had not found a way to provide children growing up in poverty an education that overcame its effects on any significant scale, and many assumed that fixing education would require fixing poverty first.

During my senior year in college, a hit movie, *Stand and Deliver*, made a national hero of Jaime Escalante, a teacher in East Los Angeles who coached a class of students to pass the AP Calculus exam. At the time, it seemed stunning that a teacher could get kids in a high-poverty community to excel at that level—so stunning that the Educational Testing Service questioned the validity of the test results of Escalante's students, creating the drama that attracted the attention of Hollywood. Movie audiences around the country were moved by the depiction of a charismatic and heroic teacher who could miraculously beat the odds with his students. We saw Escalante as an outlier—not as an example that could be widely replicated.

There was another hit movie around the same time, *Lean on Me*, which featured the efforts of a school principal at Eastside High in Paterson, New Jersey, who took unorthodox measures to create a safe environment for his students—but did not fundamentally change their academic outcomes at all. Eastside High was, and continues to be, a school where academic success is the exception rather than the rule. (In September 2008, *New Jersey Monthly* ranked the school 311th out of 316 schools in the state.)[9] That we would put this school up in lights is a striking example of the prevailing ideology when the movie was made.

In the early 1990s, there were in fact a small number of widely heralded examples of schools that changed the trajectories of children growing up in poverty. One of the most acclaimed was Marva Collins's Westside Preparatory School in Chicago, which she founded as a private school in 1975, initially to educate her own children and their neighborhood friends. The school's results were extraordinary—its students, including those who had been labeled as learning disabled by their previous schools, excelled academically, and many went on to attend the nation's finest universities.[10] Yet while a handful of schools like Westside Prep were changing the lives of their students, the working assumption at the time seemed to be that if the school leaders left, the success would not continue. Indeed, in the case of Westside Prep, the school ultimately closed its doors in June 2008, citing enrollment and funding challenges.

During my senior year, I saw a growing recognition that we had to do something about the educational inequities that were threatening to undermine our position in the global community. In the fall of that year, a *Fortune* article featured a summit in the business community on this very subject.[11] "Let's stop lamenting the crisis and do something about it," exhorted one of the quoted executives. In the two decades since, educators, community leaders, business leaders, and policy makers have pioneered a number of initiatives to remedy the crisis. We have pursued all manner of reforms—curriculum overhauls, reforms in teacher education, adopt-a-school programs, class-size reduction, governance changes, school-funding initiatives, and much more. In some cases these reforms have modestly advanced our goals, in other cases not. Sadly, in aggregate, we still have not moved the needle against the achievement gap that persists along racial and socioeconomic lines.

Despite this reality, however, I see tremendous reason for optimism. Twenty years ago, we had a few visible examples of classrooms and schools in low-income communities that were changing the trajectories of children. Today, there are too many to count. In the Teach For America network alone, there are hundreds of teachers who, even in their first and second years of teaching, are proving it is possible for economically disadvantaged children to compete academically with their higher-income peers. Moreover, today dozens of communities also have growing numbers of schools that are putting whole buildings full of students on much more promising paths, year after year.

The progress is striking even in the past decade alone. In 2003 Teach For America began placing corps members in Philadelphia. Halfway through the year, we saw large numbers of our corps members there so frustrated and overwhelmed by the challenges they and their students were facing that they began to feel the situation was hopeless. I went to the region, talked with corps members and staff, and realized that we had to show our teachers evidence of what was possible. I suggested to our team that they take corps members to visit highly successful schools serving the same student population—but they couldn't find such a school in Philadelphia. Ultimately, they resorted to arranging school visits for our corps members in other cities so that they could see that success is possible. Today in Philadelphia, less than a decade later, there are at least a half-dozen exemplary schools that are putting children in the city's highest-poverty communities on a trajectory to graduate from college at much the same rate as their peers in its more privileged communities. Although we are far from providing all the children in Philadelphia with an excellent education, today there is not just one school but a growing number of schools that are showing what is possible through education. This is dramatic progress in just a few years.

In fact, in dozens of communities around the country, there are growing numbers of classrooms and growing numbers of schools that are demonstrating that we don't need to wait to fix poverty in order to ensure that all children receive an excellent education. We can partner with children and their families, in a way that is replicable, to provide an education that changes their likely paths—an education that is transformational.

Although there is certainly much more to be understood about how to provide urban and rural children with opportunities that will put them on a path to college and life success, today we do know that it is possible to provide children growing up in poverty with an education that transforms their academic outcomes and, in turn, life options. And we can describe what it takes. Unlike twenty years ago, the question today is not whether success is possible but instead whether success is "scalable." Can we develop entire school systems that provide educational opportunity for *all* students?

Even to this question, there is growing evidence that it is possible to realize significant progress. Just seven or eight years ago, New York City, Washington, D.C., and New Orleans were on virtually everyone's list of extreme microcosms of our failure to provide children with the opportunities they need and deserve. Today, while the school districts in these cities have a long way to go, each has shown that it is in fact possible to scale the success we are seeing in some classrooms and schools. Moreover, today we are witnessing unprecedented levels of policy change at the federal, state, and local levels that make it much easier to lead high-performing schools and school systems.

It is true that we have not narrowed the achievement gap that persists along racial and economic lines over the past twenty years in an aggregate sense. But today, we know it is possible to do this, and we know infinitely more than we did even a decade ago about what it will take. This is extraordinary progress that paves the way for our nation to live up to its ideals and ensure that all of our children attain the kind of education that sets them up for equal opportunity in life.

A NEW MANDATE FOR PUBLIC EDUCATION IN URBAN AND RURAL COMMUNITIES

Successful classrooms and schools and improving districts are showing us that we can provide education that is life-transforming if we commit to do so. For the most part in our country today, students leave schools on the same trajectory they were on when they entered them; very few students enter on a path to drop out and exit on a path to college. Now we know we can change this. We will need to rally the country to embrace a new mandate for urban and rural public schools—to provide transformational education. We must build within schools in economically disadvantaged communities the mission and capacity not simply to make learning opportunities available but to ensure that children actually master the skills, knowledge, and habits of mind that set them up to have a full set of life options and that ultimately put them on a different path than the one predicted by their socioeconomic background.

The source of low educational outcomes for children in low-income communities is not uncaring students and families. The roots of this problem are that children in low-income communities face extra challenges that children in high-income communities don't face. They face all the extra stresses and burdens of poverty. They are generally not surrounded by evidence that they can achieve academic success and that this will lead to success in life. And they are also much more likely to be children of color and therefore to encounter the effects of racial discrimination. These children, who have tremendous potential and need extra support to fulfill it, show up at schools that have not typically had the mission or capacity to meet their extra needs. Instead, the schools they attend typically provide the same opportunities that might be (barely) adequate for many middle-class families. Given this set of circumstances, we should expect that teachers and schools in underresourced areas who are simply fulfilling the traditional mandate of public schools will not be successful in producing equal results.

What the growing number of successful teachers, school leaders, and system leaders reveals is that we can provide children facing all the challenges of poverty with an educational experience that places them on a level playing field with children in higher-income communities. The solution isn't to "fix" teaching, or to eliminate unions, or to double education funding, or to bring technology into education, or any number of other often proposed solutions by themselves. Instead, we must redefine our educational mission as working with students and families to ensure learning and achievement at levels that change children's academic and life trajectories. And then, to accomplish this mission, we must pursue the same comprehensive set of strategies—and invest the same level of energy and discipline—that is required to accomplish ambitious ends in any organization. There is nothing elusive about this solution, but there is nothing easy about it, either—and efforts that oversimplify the issue will fail to advance the cause and, worse, serve as dangerous distractions of time and energy.

There is much we can and should do to take the pressure off schools by improving economies in rural and urban areas, upgrading social services and health services, and providing universal high-quality early education. In fact, we are seeing that some Teach For America alumni, intimately familiar with the effects of poverty on schools through their work with students and families, will help pioneer the solutions. But we cannot wait for these initiatives, especially given what we now see is possible to accomplish through education. Indeed, providing a generation of children in urban and rural communities with transformational education should prove to be a fundamental part of the solution to poverty.

A PREVIEW OF THIS BOOK

I have had the great privilege over the past twenty years to learn from many teachers, school leaders, district leaders, and policy makers who are showing us what is possible. My purpose in writing this book is to describe what they are accomplishing and to share their insights, my own observations, and the implications for our nation's effort to address educational inequity on a scale that is commensurate with the magnitude of the problem. There are many leaders and educators whose perspectives would add a great deal to this discussion, but in this book I focus on what I have learned in my own work at Teach For America, from our corps members, alumni, and other leaders in the urban and rural communities where we work.

As in other change efforts, at the core of the solution to educational inequity is leadership. Wherever there is transformational change for children, whether at the classroom, school, or system level, there is transformational leadership—individuals who believe deeply in their students, who invest them and their families in an ambitious vision of success, and who do whatever it takes to get there. Teach For America's mission is to be one source of this transformational leadership. Certainly, we are not the only source, but our corps members and alumni have played some role in the progress made over these past twenty years. An increasing number of them represent visible examples of teachers who are putting students on a different trajectory. As the founders of some of the very first high-performing charter schools (public schools empowered with flexibility over decision making in exchange for accountability for results), they pioneered the development of the school models that are putting children in urban and rural areas on a path to succeeding in and graduating from college. Many of our alumni have helped fuel the proliferation of these models as leaders and teachers in hundreds of high-performing charter schools now dotting the education landscape, while many others have worked to bring these same approaches into traditional schools. And while the reforms undertaken in communities such as New Orleans and Washington, D.C., and in the larger policy environment are a function of many forces, there is no doubt that the leadership of Teach For America alumni has been fundamental to the progress that is taking place.

I am excited to have the chance to share the insights of our corps members and alumni and our colleagues in communities across the country with a broader audience. This isn't the story of Teach For America as an organization but rather a book sharing what I have learned from those who have joined our corps and others whom we have worked alongside.

Twenty years into this effort, Teach For America corps members and alumni, and our colleagues who are working for educational excellence and equity, have proved that the vision statement that has united all of us in the Teach For America community since the beginning—the vision that one day, all children in our nation will have the opportunity to attain an excellent education—is in fact attainable. I feel so privileged to have had the opportunity to learn from them and now to be able to share their insights.

The first half of this book is about what we can learn from successful classrooms and schools and from school systems that are making significant progress in closing the achievement gap. The second half is about where we need to go from here—the distractions we need to avoid and the strategies we need to pursue to scale success and accelerate the pace of change.

1

TEACHING AS LEADERSHIP
LESSONS FROM TRANSFORMATIONAL TEACHERS

AFTER JOINING TEACH FOR AMERICA, Megan Brousseau accepted an assignment to teach biology in Morrisania, a neighborhood in the South Bronx that President Jimmy Carter once called "the worst slum in America." Megan was familiar with the discouraging statistics associated with her school's student population—and determined to help change the odds for her students. She walked into class on that first day of school in the fall of 2008 and announced to her ninth grade students that her goal was for all of them to take and pass the rigorous New York State Regents Exam, a seemingly impossible feat.

Over the summer Megan had given a lot of thought to the question of what she could accomplish with her students. She knew that if her students passed the Regents Exam in biology, they would fulfill the science requirement for receiving the prestigious State Regents

Diploma, be prepared to take the SAT II in biology, and be eligible for one of New York City's many merit-based college scholarships. She also knew the historical reality that most students in the Bronx do not take and pass this exam. "This is your chance to make history," she told her students.

Given their academic starting point, her goal was ambitious to say the least. In her first week Megan found that many of her students lacked even basic knowledge of the eighth grade material they were supposed to have mastered the year before. Consulting with her colleagues in the English Department, she found that 60 percent of her students were below grade level in English, with 20 percent more than three grades behind. For most of her students, English was a second language, with only Spanish spoken at home. When she took stock of the situation, Megan was "reeling."

Considering the stakes for her students, however, she kept at it. Nine months and an immense amount of hard work later, all but 3 of her 112 students passed the Regents Exam on their first try. Her students boasted an average score of 81 percent, higher than the citywide average of 72 percent, which includes the results at New York's prestigious specialized high schools. Her other 3 students passed on a second try after additional tutoring from Megan.

For each of Megan's students, passing the Regents meant something unique. For one of her most advanced students, who constantly challenged Megan to teach him more, scoring a 94 percent on the test was the first step in achieving his dream of becoming a pediatric oncologist. Another student—a shy, mildly autistic girl who entered Megan's class reading at a fourth grade level and scoring a 9 percent on the diagnostic assessment—passed with a 68 percent. She approached Megan after she got her results and simply said, "I know I can do it now. . . . Thank you."

At the same time that Megan was starting her teaching commitment in the Bronx, Maurice Thomas was beginning to teach eleventh grade history in Atlanta. Maurice's course would end in a Georgia High School Graduation Test covering all social studies material from ninth to eleventh grades. His students would have to pass in order to graduate—a tall order for a class that, the previous year, had been taught by a permanent substitute teacher.

When Maurice diagnosed his students' academic skills at the beginning of the year, he found that they had mastered, on average, only 67 percent of the standards they were supposed to have learned in the ninth and tenth grades and that half of his juniors were reading below an eighth grade level. The more Maurice reflected on this situation, the more indignant he became. "I was angry because my students had been failed," he said. "I realized that I had to be the one to stop the cycle. I was filled with a sense of urgency." He described the challenge: "Teaching in Southwest Atlanta presents a unique set of challenges for my students and me. The neighborhood of Ben Hill that surrounds my school is filled with crime, teen pregnancy, and poverty. All of these factors make their way into our school every day. Of the twenty-two girls I taught last year, ten were pregnant or had children. Many believed that they could not achieve— that the poverty and crime of the neighborhood would force them to limit their career paths in order to find quick money to provide for their children."

One day early in the year, Maurice told his students a story about a young girl who had attended his own high school in Milwaukee, Wisconsin. She was a typical student in most respects, but in her junior year she had a baby boy. Her father was an alcoholic and wasn't supportive of her, and she considered dropping out, but in the end she did not quit. She came to school every day, sometimes with the baby. In fact, she went to summer school to take classes and graduated a full semester before the rest of the senior class. She enrolled in the local college and majored in nursing. In two years she graduated with a degree and was a registered nurse. She is now happily married with four kids and doing just fine. "This woman who never gave up, who never made excuses, was my mother, and that baby was me, your teacher," he told his students. By sharing his own story, and in many other ways, Maurice went about investing his students in the goal of passing the year-end exam and in his belief that "college was the only option."

After an enormous amount of hard work on his part and on the part of his students, all of them passed the exam needed to graduate, and a year later he saw them all—fifty-five high school seniors—gain admission to college. Some are attending junior colleges; many are going to four-year colleges including Georgia State, Clark Atlanta University, Agnes Scott College, and the University of Kentucky, some with scholarships worth as much as sixty-five thousand dollars.

○ ○ ○

IN 1990 THE FIRST TEACH FOR AMERICA corps of almost 500 teachers headed into classrooms across the country, fueled by seemingly unlimited energy and idealism. They had been selected from among the 2,500 college seniors who had applied to Teach For America in response to a grassroots recruitment campaign—flyers under doors—orchestrated by our founding team. These pioneering corps members embraced their challenging assignments, determined to make a difference in their students' lives. The work proved extremely difficult, both for our teachers and for our nascent organization. As I spent time in the classrooms of many of our teachers during those first few years, I was humbled by their work ethic and their commitment to their students, but I was also painfully aware that we were not having the impact we had originally envisioned. For the most part I met teachers who were working valiantly to deliver engaging lesson plans but were exhausted by the classroom management challenges, the administrative requirements of teaching, and the emotional drain of seeing their students struggle with weighty problems outside the classroom. Though they shared an intense desire to do right by their students, many of our corps members struggled to have the sort of profound impact on students' lives that we all knew was necessary. For some of our teachers, simply surviving became the goal.

When I would ask our teachers what they were working on, or what they were aiming toward, I would hear a range of answers. For some, the emphasis seemed to be mostly on their own development as teachers ("I'm working to become a better writing teacher"). Others said they would be happy if they could truly "reach one child." Still others defined success as inspiring a love of learning. Some of the most ambitious of our teachers were undertaking dramatic feats to expand students' horizons or to engage them in serving their communities. We had teachers working hard on everything from creating and running chess clubs to taking groups of students to France to painting over graffiti on campus walls. Principals were giving most of our teachers high marks.

But I began hearing about a few teachers who were having an entirely different level of impact, whose accomplishments astonished even longtime education veterans. I set out to learn what they were doing differently. In the spring of 1996 I went up to the Bronx to spend some time with David Levin. Today, Dave is best known for founding, along with fellow Teach For America alumnus Mike Feinberg, the Knowledge Is Power Program (KIPP), a highly successful network of charter schools across the country. In the mid-1990s, he was one of the teachers I was hearing so much about.

His students, fifth graders coming from the same challenging backgrounds as the millions who were falling behind and dropping out, were performing well academically on an absolute scale. It was clear that Dave was having a transformational impact on their lives.

I spent several days watching Dave teach. The more I observed, the more I realized how different his classroom was from so many that might be considered "good" by conventional criteria. Dave's students were not just "on task." They were on a mission to go to college, and Dave was on a mission to get them there.

Dave asked his students and their parents to work hard in order to get on track to go to college, and he pledged to do whatever it took to help them succeed. He spent a good deal of his time convincing his students that if they worked hard enough, they would "get smart" and that this would matter in their lives. In math, language arts, and social studies, I saw Dave building a culture of hard work and achievement as he stood below banners that read "There are no shortcuts" and "Team beats individual." I still remember the lack of air conditioning in Dave's school on one ninety-six-degree day when I visited. Dave's response was to reinforce the belief that no obstacle is insurmountable, no excuse acceptable. "The heat is not going to stop us from thinking," he said, and indeed, his students were so engrossed they seemed virtually unfazed by the weather.

There was a sense of urgency in Dave's room as his students absorbed math concepts and discussed novels. He was maximizing every minute to move his students from one point to another. He did not appear to employ a singular instructional approach. As he told me at the time, "We're looking for things that work." During his math class, which I remember to this day, the students were so engaged that they forgot they were cutting into their time for PE. After talking through one of the thinking-skills problems and a lesson on changing fractions into percentages, Dave had begun a contest. It was so much fun that I found myself competing with the kids. The gym teacher, who had come to the class to pick up the kids for PE, asked Dave if she could participate after watching for ten minutes.

Dave's students were showing up at least forty-five minutes early for extra instruction and then staying after school for two hours Monday through Thursday. They were coming five hours a day on Saturdays and for four weeks of summer school.

I had never seen a teacher like this before. Reflecting on my own experience growing up and attending a public school in a privileged community in Dallas—a community that calls itself the "bubble" for its lack of diversity and disadvantage—a few of my teachers stood out as having particularly high expectations, but many of them seemed driven mostly to get through the material. They knew that if they did a good job, some of their students would truly master the material, some would do so at an average level, and most of the rest would at least retain enough to move to the next grade. The teachers cared about us, and they made a difference in our lives, but more often than not, they defined their roles as giving students an opportunity to access new skills and knowledge by putting the material in front of them.

This worked out in my school, where all of us showed up having fully internalized from our parents the expectation that "of course" we would go to college. Just about all of our parents had. Sure enough, 97 percent of my graduating high school class went off to college, most to selective colleges.[1] Our teachers had succeeded by most standards, and many had had a real impact on us, but they didn't change our life trajectories per se. For the most part, we entered school on a trajectory and accessed the opportunities to continue on that trajectory.

In Dave, I saw a teacher who was determined that every one of his students would thoroughly master the material. He had a long-term goal that involved changing his students' expected trajectories, and he redefined the role of teacher and the nature of school itself to get there. This was transformational teaching.

Seeing what Dave Levin was accomplishing—and recognizing similarities between his approach and that of several other teachers who were also attaining notable success—gave me and my colleagues a sense of possibility that many more of our corps members might be capable of achieving similar results. We set out to systematically study teachers attaining demonstrable success and to channel what we learned into our methods for selecting, training, and supporting corps members.

○ ○ ○

OVER THE PAST TWENTY YEARS, and even more quickly over the past decade, we have seen the number of highly effective teachers like Dave in our corps grow considerably. Teachers with diverse cultural backgrounds and personalities, across all grade levels and subjects, are changing the lives of their students. Spending time with them reveals striking patterns and lessons, about the nature of transformational teaching and about educational inequity and its solutions. In the pages that follow, I'll attempt to bring a few of their stories to life and then step back to share the lessons I take from their examples and others like them.

Let's start with Megan Brousseau and her determination that her students "make history" by outperforming some of the highest-performing classrooms in the state. When I visited her class during her second year, her freshmen were only weeks away from the Regents Exam. She started off the lesson with a four-minute clip of a coach (played by Al Pacino) giving his professional football team an intense and inspiring half-time speech in the movie *Any Given Sunday*: "The inches we need are everywhere around us. On this team we fight for that inch!" screamed Pacino. The clip was enough to give me my dose of inspiration for the day, and I could see the impact on the students. Megan seamlessly transitioned to her own PowerPoint slide show and pregame rally. Picking up on the coach's theme that success was going to mean scraping for every last inch of progress, she encouraged her students to maximize every possible moment and put forth every ounce of energy to reach their goal.

Megan had gone to great lengths to invest her students in the idea that passing this exam would make a meaningful difference in their lives and that they could in fact do it. She asked her students to follow the simple rules "be prompt, polite, and prepared" and to live by the class motto: "Your Choices + Your Actions = Your Future. Choose Your Future." She put this motto on every paper she handed to students. From what I could see, students were acting on that sentiment. They were at every turn embracing the hard work of engaging deeply with rigorous content.

Megan's frequent assessments of her students' progress enabled her to give students a sense of ownership over their learning. In order to understand how much of the daily lesson her students had mastered, she designed a daily ritual called "Rapid Fire." Rapid Fire was the three- to five-minute closing at the end of class. She pulled a name out of a basket; the student had to stand up, listen to the question, and answer without using notes.

To provide stepping-stones before each major unit assessment, she gave quizzes every Friday. The quizzes were composed of old Regents questions, vocabulary questions, and usually one free response. Those students who scored 85 percent or above on the most recent assessment or who made at least an 8 percent improvement over their previous assessment became part of an "exclusive club." Members of that club earned the right to choose their seats instead of being assigned to them and earned one homework pass for each week of membership.

After every unit test, all of her students filled out a tracker, enabling them to set goals and develop plans for meeting them. These assessments also ensured Megan was maximizing her time with her students and advancing them toward the big goal. She rolled up the data to inform her lesson plans. She would spend hours dividing students into groups that would enable her to differentiate instruction effectively—and she changed the composition of those groups frequently, depending on student needs. The morning I visited, she had one table that was entirely composed of students who had very low reading levels and a variety of learning disorders. She could sit and work with this group exclusively for fifteen minutes during independent practice, while knowing the rest of the class would be able to complete the work without her assistance.

Every element of Megan's classroom was purposefully planned and thoughtfully implemented to foster students' deep engagement with hard ideas and to ensure her learning objectives were actually being met. Not only did Megan seem to know precisely what should be happening at every moment in the classroom, but all of her actions seemed to be designed to further her aim of student learning, from the detailed lesson plans and unit plans to the well-practiced systems for walking in the door (greeting Megan with a handshake, direct eye contact, and a formal "Good morning"; depositing homework; and starting immediately to work on the "brain buster"), handling tardy students (students simply wrote their name on a clipboard as they walked in, and Megan followed up with a call to their families that same day), and catching up on homework after an absence (the homework was available in a folder). Every minute in the classroom was treated as precious by teacher and students alike.

On the day I visited her room, after the Pacino-inspired motivational start, I, like the students, was drawn into Megan's engaging review. She led the class in a rousing game of "Two Truths and a Lie," in which teams of students tried to stump other teams with their knowledge of human biology, and every truth or lie had to be probed, explained, and understood.

I watched as students reviewed the most difficult concepts they had studied, drawing from the rich and creative learning experiences they had had. There was the day Megan showed up in scrubs and designated certain students as patients with ailments that others had to diagnose, using their knowledge of body systems. There was the day the class created and presented thirty-second commercials out of what they had learned about enzyme synthesis and digestion. There was the day Megan told them that a new species had shown up at the Bronx Zoo and they had to debate whether a rain forest or desert habitat was appropriate based on the creature's adaptive features.

In the morning while she got ready for work, Megan would make ten to fifteen wake-up calls to students in her first-period class to make sure they were awake and planned to be at school on time. Even with all her students present and her extraordinary time-management skills, Megan was still not able to spend enough time with individual students to bring them up to grade level. So she would tutor from 7:30 A.M. until the beginning of first period and again during lunch. At the end of the day she would walk around the building to collect her students for after-school tutoring sessions that generally wound up around 6:00. In the spring, when she realized that her students needed additional review time, she started a Saturday school session. Her principal agreed to open the school, and Megan called the homes of eighty students and asked their parents to please help convince their son or daughter to attend Saturday Academy. She talked to each student individually and explained why it was so important to give up a few precious hours of the weekend. The first Saturday seventy-six of her eighty students were at the front door of the school at 8:30 A.M. Although the attendance fluctuated somewhat due to family situations and prior commitments, she never had fewer than sixty-five students in Saturday Academy for any of the six weeks leading up to the Regents.

Watching Megan lead her classroom, I was reminded of Dave Levin. They had different styles and instructional techniques, but they shared a deep sense of purpose. They were on a mission, and they had gotten their students on a mission. They were maximizing the value of every available second, and when that wasn't enough to reach their desired outcomes, they found the additional time necessary to give their students what they needed to succeed.

Megan, like Dave, was a transformational teacher—changing the predicted outcomes for her students.

While Megan's students were making history in New York, Maurice's were doing the same in Atlanta. When I went to visit Maurice, I found him with his students in a room that was once three closets, in a school that was under construction. A red badger, the University of Wisconsin mascot, stared up at me from a poster on the door. As I walked into the room and settled at a desk in the back, I saw two handwritten posters announcing Maurice's vision for his students. The first said:

BIG GOAL: 80% CLASS MASTERY!!
Including Exit Tickets,
Quizzes, Tests, Essays, and Projects.

The second poster said:

BIGGER GOAL:
ALL OF US WILL GO TO COLLEGE!!
THE LUCKY ONES
WILL ATTEND WISCONSIN!!

Indicators of his success in investing students in working hard to reach these goals were everywhere—starting with the fact that neither Maurice nor his students seemed to notice I had entered the room. They were absolutely absorbed in a student-led discussion of the relevance and legacy of *Brown v. Board of Education* and Dr. King's "I have a dream" speech. Students were leaning forward, emphatically making their points—each new point provoking additional impassioned agreement and disagreement.

In front of me at the "observers' table" were Maurice's thoughtful lesson plans. Using classroom discussions and college-level writing assignments based on primary sources, Maurice was moving his students toward high-rigor objectives related to both content knowledge and critical thinking. As I watched the plans play out before my eyes, I saw Maurice deftly redirect and guide his students' thinking.

After thirty minutes that seemed like ten, the class ended, and I had a chance to talk to Maurice. "Once I decided that everyone was going to college, it changed everything," he told me. "When they come to me, they are mostly not on track to college. Many are reading on a sixth grade level. They don't have the social skills they need. They don't have research skills, they can't analyze and synthesize—they can't do all these things you need to do to go to and succeed in college. This is not kindergarten, and we don't have twelve years to fix this. I've got twelve months to get this done if they are going to college. Twelve months. We have to get to *work*. So it really puts a lot of pressure on me to give them everything they need."

Maurice began to list the ways in which he has gone above and beyond conventional expectations to ensure his students realize the "bigger goal" of college. He takes students (alternating boys and girls each month) on college visits. ("My kids live in Atlanta, surrounded by great universities, and most of them have never stepped foot on a college campus," he told me.) He tutors students before and after school for ACT and SAT preparation. Maurice holds well-attended weekly "town meetings" with upperclassmen and their families to check in on college applications, financial aid progress, and challenges that he can help address.

Informed by his review of rigorous history curricula, Maurice changed his traditional high school social studies course into a college-like seminar that developed certain skills and abilities. He engaged his students in analyzing historical texts, critiquing different points of view, developing research skills, and thinking analytically. He expected his students to complete a 1,500-word research paper on a historical topic of their choice.

Like Megan Brousseau, Maurice found that the use of visual tracking was key in getting his students invested in their own progress. Each class period culminated in exit tickets built from tough questions aligned with the lesson's objectives, and Maurice created an exit-ticket tracker that allowed students to see, in an instant, their success on those daily assessments. Students who earned 80 percent mastery on the exit ticket were recognized and celebrated. Maurice said he was initially skeptical that this would work with seventeen-year-old students. But later he changed his mind:

> Not only did the tracker invest students in their academic goal, it also helped to create a healthy competition around scholarship and a culture of success in my class. Students would applaud the success of others and began to reteach and clear up misconceptions about the content material immediately after grading exit tickets. They were taking ownership of Room 313 and, more important, ownership of their learning. They were the masters. After this small victory, I went wild with trackers. Soon I had trackers of unit tests and homework.

During winter break of his first year, Maurice's principal called to inform him that she wanted him to serve as the eleventh grade team leader. "I told her no, and she kindly explained that she was in charge and that I would be team leader," he laughed. Suddenly, Maurice felt responsible not just for his individual classroom but for the entire eleventh grade. The gradewide performance on the eleventh grade English and math exams, which would determine the school's Adequate Yearly Progress (a federal designation of school progress known as AYP), was placed on his shoulders.

In January Maurice gave the juniors a mock exam and found that fewer than half of his students were on track to mastery in English and math. With only three months until the test, Maurice realized he had to make radical changes. He gave students new class schedules and assigned them to cohorts based on their math scores. Students were placed into three groups, with the lowest-performing group on a schedule that included three hours of math instruction every day. Most students attended mandatory tutorials and four-hour Saturday sessions.

Maurice's leadership was transformational for his students and indeed for the whole school. At the end of the year, Maurice's was one of six Atlanta public high schools to meet federal expectations for AYP out of the eighteen high schools in the district. Ninety-four percent of his school's students passed the Georgia High School Graduation Test in math, and 81 percent passed in English.

While Megan and Maurice were both teaching at the high school level, visits to dramatically successful teachers at any grade level reveal similar patterns. When Priscilla Mendoza first met her second graders at Dr. Bernard Black Elementary School in Phoenix, they were reading on average at a mid–first grade level and had mastered fewer than one-third of first grade math objectives. The struggles of Priscilla's students reflected those of the school more generally. Proficiency levels hovered around 50 percent, and on average students were in the bottom third in academic performance compared to national norms.[2]

Seeing how far behind her students were, she determined to put them on a different trajectory. She set out to advance her students two years in a year's time so that they were ready to enter third grade on or above grade level. Priscilla said that she knew this would be possible because "when she wants something, she finds a way to make it happen," and she set out to inspire the same sense of possibility within her students.

Drawing on her love of international travel and language and culture, she referred to her second graders as the Brilliant Backpackers and aligned everything with her classroom theme of traveling the world. Her motto was "Work hard. Get smart. Go far." When students collectively achieved a class average of 85 percent or higher on her rigorous assessments, they were able to "travel" to a new country. For each "trip," Priscilla transformed her room into a colorful, warm, and engaging celebration of a new country's culture and language.

Priscilla made her students' performance objectives as transparent as possible by listing them on the board daily and referring to them throughout their lessons. She worked with each student during an individual weekly conference to set a new goal for their reading. Student progress was tracked on colorful wall displays, and students took ownership of their learning by grading and tracking their assessments on bar graphs in their very own "Passports." Their passports became their "tickets" to a new country.

Priscilla communicated regularly with her students' parents, explaining her goals and how they could support the children's effort. She reached out to each family by phone at least twice a month, welcomed them into her classroom, and spent time with them outside of the classroom at any and all birthday parties and sporting events she was invited to.

Priscilla's days were as purposeful as Megan's and Maurice's. An average day in her classroom consisted of a series of seven- to ten-minute lessons interspersed between work sessions each lasting approximately twenty-five minutes. She used the state standards as well as district curricula to organize her lessons and created small groups of students that changed based on the subject and skill and enabled Priscilla to meet their individual needs.

And, also like Megan and Maurice, she reached far beyond her school's resource constraints in order to meet her students' extra needs. When she encountered obstacles, which she often did, she went to great lengths to overcome them. Priscilla collected leftover breakfast bars and cereal packs to distribute to students at the end of the day. For several students who were tardy or even absent on a regular basis, she established daily contact with their parents and checked in if these students had not arrived by the end of breakfast. She sought out siblings, stayed late for parents, sometimes even delivered schoolwork to students who missed school. She conducted a book drive that resulted in a classroom library of one thousand books. Noting several students' lack of books at home, she gave a minimum of twenty student-selected books to each student. In addition to books, Priscilla raised thousands of dollars for classroom supplies and for an after-school art program. She often sent students home with pencils and paper as needed. She rewarded those students who scored 100 percent on an assessment with lunch and a piano lesson—given how much her students were achieving, she found herself at the piano bench with a student four days a week.

By the end of the year Priscilla's students had met their goals, and three-quarters of them ended the year reading on a third grade level, progress that left her students on a very different academic trajectory than the one they were on at the beginning of the year. Her students ended the year with dreams and plans of traveling the world someday, driven by a sense of endless possibility.

○ ○ ○

WHAT I'VE LEARNED FROM DAVE, Megan, Maurice, Priscilla, and other teachers like them has shaped my convictions about the problem of educational inequity and its solutions. I take three main lessons from their examples.

LESSON 1:
SUCCESS IS POSSIBLE IN CLASSROOMS
IN LOW-INCOME COMMUNITIES

What is most striking about these examples is that they show us what is possible. If Megan can ensure students (including those starting the year reading at a fourth grade level) go on to pass a ninth grade Regents Exam, Maurice can put high school juniors reading on an eighth grade level on a path to graduating from high school and gaining college admission, and Priscilla can accelerate her students who start out so far behind so that they end the second grade on average ahead of grade level, then, clearly, we can solve the problem of educational inequity through efforts centered within schools.

Megan, Maurice, and Priscilla show us that it is possible to do this *if we redefine the role of the teacher* to mean more than providing access to learning experiences. Instead, these teachers set out to inspire their students to assume responsibility for meeting ambitious academic goals, and they commit to doing whatever it takes to ensure their students succeed—providing the academic rigor and the extra supports necessary to meet their extra needs. They show us that teachers who redefine their roles don't need to wait to solve poverty before their students can fulfill their potential. Rather, they can partner with children and their families to provide an education that is transformational for them, an education that changes their likely path and enables them to "make history," to use Megan's words. This is the most salient lesson of our work.

LESSON 2:
TRANSFORMATIONAL TEACHING IS
TRANSFORMATIONAL LEADERSHIP

Every time we study teachers who are having a profound impact on the opportunities facing children growing up in low-income communities, we find teachers who operate like the most effective leaders in any context. They establish an ambitious vision for their students' success that will make a difference in their academic and life trajectories. They invest others—students and their families—in this vision and in working hard to reach it. They are purposeful and strategic in moving toward it, constantly evaluating their students' progress and making adjustments to ensure their success. When they encounter obstacles, they do whatever it takes to overcome them, exerting extraordinary time, energy, and resourcefulness. They reflect on their accomplishments and shortcomings, seek and find help from veteran teachers and other colleagues, and improve over time.

Megan, Maurice, and Priscilla each identified powerful motivating visions and goals that would make a meaningful difference for their students. In Megan's case, passing the Regents Exam in ninth grade would enable students to be placed into advanced classes that would put them on a college track. For Maurice's students, passing the year-end exam was a prerequisite for high school completion, and gaining college admission was a first step to different prospects than those awaiting the vast majority of Atlanta's children. For Priscilla's students, entering third grade ahead of grade level meant that teachers would begin seeing them as gifted and talented, which would influence the perceptions and expectations they would encounter thereafter. Embracing meaningful, motivating goals can be powerful in any context. Ambitious goals create a sense of urgency, shared focus, and alignment of action that accelerates progress. In schools in our low-income communities, where there often isn't an expectation of the highest levels of academic achievement—because there isn't clear and ever-present evidence that it is possible or that it pays off—ambitious goal setting is a crucial element of transformative teaching.

Beyond goal setting, Megan, Maurice, and Priscilla all employed extremely sophisticated strategies to inspire their students to work harder than they'd ever worked in order to reach their goals. By showing students exactly where they were in relation to their goals, and empowering them to track and manage their own progress, they instilled a new level of personal ownership for success among their students. In the context of urban and rural communities, where students are unlikely to consistently encounter classrooms and schools that meet their needs, teachers have to exert extra effort to ensure that students understand that their education and ultimate success are products of their own resilience and hard work—that while it may be unfair, attaining their goals will require greater effort. Through personal relationships, constantly reinforcing messages about the importance of hard work and personal responsibility for success, charging students with tracking their own progress, and engaging students' families, these teachers are able to get their students on a mission to beat the odds.

We also see that successful teaching requires the same skill in planning and effective execution that is commonly expected of successful leaders in any context. Megan, Maurice, and Priscilla were each obsessed with understanding where their students were against their goals at any given point and using that information to inform sophisticated plans to meet their students' different needs. These teachers brought intensity to their classrooms each day, maximizing each moment in the effort to move their students ahead, changing and adjusting course as necessary.

Additionally, transformational teaching requires immense resourcefulness, time, and energy, just as great leadership in any setting does. Children growing up in poverty face enormous challenges—often including lack of adequate nutrition, health care, housing, and high-quality preschool programs, for example. Because children in low-income communities are disproportionately children of color, they are also more likely to encounter the effects of societal low expectations and discrimination. These children show up at schools that don't have the resources to meet their extra needs. Changing their trajectories requires reaching far beyond traditional conceptions of teaching to access the time and resources necessary to meet students' extra needs and to make up for the lack of capacity of today's schools. Thus, we saw how Megan worked to spend more time with her students, what Maurice did to orient his students and their families to the expectations of college, and what Priscilla did to garner extra resources for her class.

In sum, successful teaching in urban and rural areas requires all the same approaches that transformational leadership in any setting requires. It requires extraordinary energy, discipline, and hard work. What is encouraging is that there is nothing elusive about it. We can replicate and spread success. By deepening our understanding of what differentiates the most successful teachers and feeding those lessons into strategies for selection, training, and professional development, we can increase the number of highly successful teachers.

Teach For America has been deeply engaged in this endeavor for years now. Given what it takes to be successful, we know we must begin with people who have the personal characteristics associated with successful leadership. We have worked to isolate the characteristics that we can see at the selection stage that predict our teachers' success and have built an intensive admissions process to identify those most likely to succeed. (The most predictive traits are characteristics such as past demonstrated achievement, perseverance, the ability to influence and motivate others, critical thinking skills, and organizational ability.) Moreover, understanding the approaches that are common across our most successful teachers has led to the development of the Teaching As Leadership framework and support curriculum, which is now the foundation for our teacher preparation and professional development program. Understanding much more about what is involved in successful teaching, we are investing significantly in developing the necessary mindsets, skills, and knowledge through preservice and ongoing professional development.

Given the patterns we see in highly effective teachers' classrooms, we know that many more teachers—teachers who are merely "good" right now—can in fact be great, achieving a more meaningful and lasting impact in students' lives. The pervasive perspective that great teaching is magic, and not replicable, is simply not true, and it must not hold us back from cultivating teaching approaches that result in dramatic results for students.

LESSON 3:
THE LIMITS OF HEROIC TEACHING

At the same time that these teachers are showing how many more teachers can have a meaningful impact, they are also showing us that heroic teaching like theirs does not offer a likely path to educational opportunity for all. It is impossible to imagine a force of hundreds of thousands of teachers as rare in their abilities and commitment as Megan and Maurice are, and it is impossible to imagine hundreds of thousands of them sustaining the requisite level of energy and devoting the requisite amount of time not just for two years but for many years, and on a teacher's salary to boot. We can't expect all of our teachers to shoulder the responsibility of creating transformational classrooms within schools that often don't have the mission or capacity to change students' trajectories, let alone provide teachers with the training and professional development necessary to teach this way.

Our own experience at Teach For America bears this out. To be clear, these examples represent the very best of our teachers. Despite years of research and observation, millions of dollars, and the attention of the best minds we could find, we are still working to produce even a relatively small force of teachers who are consistently effecting the level of student progress that we saw in the classrooms of Megan, Maurice, and Priscilla. Yet we would need hundreds of thousands more to close the achievement gap.

At Teach For America we always aspire to be better than we currently are, and we do believe that—in light of what we are learning from highly effective teachers—we can improve to the point where we have a leadership force of teachers who are much more consistently highly successful, even in the most challenging of environments. We believe it is important to persist in this work for the sake of kids growing up today. We also believe that by realizing their full potential as successful teachers, our corps members will become more effective long-term leaders and advocates for the changes necessary to scale success.

But ultimately, the sustainable solution to educational inequity will involve building systems around teachers that support the approaches and outcomes we see in classrooms like Dave's, Megan's, Maurice's, and Priscilla's. As we'll see in subsequent chapters, we can create transformational schools that are centered around a vision of academic and life success, inspire student investment and achievement, provide the necessary resources and time, and ensure the professional development necessary to enable capable, committed teachers—but not absolute superheroes—to serve children well.

○ ○ ○

MEGAN CHALLENGED HER STUDENTS to make history, and they did. They showed that they could overcome the challenges of poverty, and the stereotypes of children of color, to defy the odds. In the process, Megan has shown us that we can make history, too. We can achieve our goal of providing children in our most economically disadvantaged communities with an education that is transformational for them. Accomplishing this isn't magic or elusive, but it isn't easy, either.

A couple of years ago, in a particularly striking example of the impact of transformational teaching, a group of Teach For America corps members and non–Teach For America teachers in the small border town of Roma, Texas, worked together to bring their students to Harvard for a college visit. The teachers and students had spent countless evenings selling nachos at middle school volleyball games, reaching out to local businesses, and hosting various events to raise funds for the trip. The teachers (and a Teach For America alumna who was a principal) raised money by reaching out to friends and relatives as well. Having grown up in one of the poorest counties in the country, many of the students had never been out of Texas except to Mexico, and most of those who had traveled did so as migrant workers picking or canning fruit with their families in other states during the summer. Most had never been on an airplane.

A number of Teach For America alumni at Harvard graduate schools rallied to host the students. Our recruitment director at Harvard at the time, Josh Biber (who himself had been a phenomenal teacher in our corps in Phoenix and is now our executive director in Boston), hosted one event in which he essentially put the Roma high school students in charge. He brought together a group of Harvard undergrads who were considering joining Teach For America and asked the Roma students to tell these college students what qualities they wanted to see in a great teacher. The Harvard students introduced themselves to the Roma students, going around the circle and announcing where they were from and what their majors were. Josh had asked them to tell when they would graduate, and each of them ended with "I will graduate from Harvard in 2009" or "I will graduate from Harvard in 2010."

When the Harvard students' self-introductions were finished, a Roma high school student stood up and introduced himself. With great confidence, he announced, "My name is Heberto. I'm a junior at Roma High School, and I will be graduating from Harvard in 2012." The room exploded with laughter and applause, but Heberto wasn't finished. He surveyed all the potential future teachers and spoke directly to them: "I want a teacher who will challenge me. I want a teacher who has high expectations for the work I can achieve. I want teachers, and I want you all to become teachers, who will believe in our potential, no matter what. Even on the days when we act like we don't want to learn, I want teachers who won't stop pushing us to be the best we can." And then he pointed at Zach Blattner, one of the teachers who had put the trip together. "I want teachers like Mr. Blattner. Mr. Blattner has me reading Kafka." Heberto saw doubt on their faces, so he reached in his backpack and whipped out *The Metamorphosis and Other Stories*. "I'm on page 98—see?" The Harvard students broke into applause.

Heberto and his classmates' trip to Harvard was just one vignette in an ongoing story of the transformational power of strong leaders in the Rio Grande Valley—both within and outside of Teach For America—who are investing students, their families, and their community in a vision of transformational change. Just five or six years earlier, when Teach For America was placing few if any teachers in the relatively isolated town of Roma, the area's top-performing students (in terms of grade point average) were either not going to college or attending a two-year vocation-focused college. A few went to the University of Texas–Pan American down the highway in the Rio Grande Valley. For students in Roma, college was just not an expected step in one's education, and few imagined attending a selective institution outside of the vicinity.

A steady stream of corps members teaching in Roma have insisted on rigorous college-focused instruction in subjects like AP English. Their work helped lead to the first Roma students passing advanced placement exams in a number of courses, including literature, English, U.S. history, and world history. Some of these teachers ran after-school ACT and SAT preparation courses for Roma students and helped focus students on college-ready writing skills.

Today, high-achieving students in Roma—thanks in part to the support, mentoring, academic instruction, and guidance from Teach For America teachers—have more options and possibilities than they once had. Roma has sent students to top-ranked universities all over the United States and Mexico. In the past few years, its top graduates have headed off to the likes of Harvard, Brown, Duke, Vassar, the University of Houston, the State University of New York, Austin College, and Georgetown.

As I was writing this book, I was forwarded an e-mail that Heberto sent to some of the Teach For America staff members who had hosted him on that college trip four years earlier:

> *I will be a junior at Harvard this coming academic year and I am concentrating in Economics and fulfilling my pre-med requirements. With this, I plan to graduate with an MD/MBA in the future and practice medicine for a while and then maybe go into health care or hospital management. Junior year should be a tough year since I will be taking the hardest Economics requirement and Organic Chemistry during the fall. I will just have to work extra hard! Either way, I digress! Harvard has been amazing and I do not regret choosing Harvard and never will. It has given me so much—friends (more like a family), great opportunities, knowledge, etc. In fact, because of Harvard's resources, I studied abroad in Venice, Italy this past summer and will be implementing a water purification system in an indigenous village in Bolivia probably next summer. I just love it!*

Heberto ended his e-mail with a postscript: He is considering joining Teach For America before going to medical school.

Teachers like Zach Blattner show us how possible and powerful it would be to reach our goal of educational opportunity for all. Ultimately, we will need to introduce critical contextual changes to make these teachers' efforts more manageable, more sustainable, and more scaleable.

2

NO SHORTCUTS

LESSONS FROM TRANSFORMATIONAL SCHOOLS

CHRIS BARBIC TAUGHT SIXTH GRADE in Houston as a member of Teach For America in 1992. His students made dramatic progress, outpacing most other students across the city. The next year he and his students' families watched with dismay as his former sixth graders' progress stalled and reversed once they entered seventh grade. A group of concerned parents, teachers, and community leaders gathered to discuss the problem. They were distraught about the gang activity, drug abuse, and teenage pregnancy prevalent in the local middle school. Having seen the power of high expectations in Chris's classroom, they dreaded surrendering their children to the culture of failure.

At the parent group's urging, Chris asked the school board for space at Rusk Elementary that would enable him to keep working with the sixth graders he had taught through eighth grade, so they would not have to transfer to the failing school. Three hundred parents and students packed the room at a Houston Independent School District (HISD) school board meeting to advocate for the plan. The mobilization worked. Chris was granted space at Rusk Elementary School to start his own school, YES College Preparatory.

Driven by his deep conviction that his students were as capable as students in any other community, Chris created this school around the vision that all of his students, not just some and certainly not the tiny fraction that statistics would predict, would go to college. Chris's vision was that his students would grow up to be intelligent, confident, critical thinkers who would recognize their ability to make the world a better place. "YES" stands for "Youth Engaged in Service," reflecting Chris's vision of YES Prep students returning to Houston armed with college degrees and determined to make a positive difference.

Today, Chris describes the school's mission simply: "We want to produce good, intelligent people who have lots of choices in life." He wants to prove that the average kid in a low-income community can succeed in college, in the same way that an average kid in a high-income community is likely to succeed in college. YES Prep currently serves 3,500 children in Houston, 90 percent of whom will be the first generation in their families to go to college, 80 percent of whom are economically disadvantaged, and 96 percent of whom are Latino or African American.

After just three years of operation, Chris's school, by then housed in several trailers in the middle of a parking lot, received the state's highest ranking ("exemplary") for school effectiveness.[1] And while less than half of Houston's low-income African American and Hispanic students graduate from high school,[2] and 10 percent graduate from college,[3] Chris reports that all YES alumni have graduated from high school, and 82 percent have graduated from or are still enrolled in college—which means they are outperforming students in the top family-income quartile nationally.[4] In 2010, for the tenth consecutive year, *every single graduate* had been accepted to a four-year college. Among the schools accepting YES Prep graduates are Harvard, Yale, Columbia, Rice, Stanford, and the University of Texas at Austin. YES Prep students have earned nearly $28 million in scholarships and financial aid.

YES Prep currently operates seven campuses; each campus starts with one class and "grows up," adding a new grade every year as its oldest students advance toward college. YES Prep schools are free and open enrollment. Families in the neighborhood are seeing what's happening at the school and are rushing to sign their children up; for their established schools, there are roughly three to four applicants for every spot, and a lottery is in place to randomly accept students. When its fifth campus begins graduating seniors in 2014, YES Prep will be sending roughly the same number of low-income students to college as all of HISD's other thirty-four high schools combined, unless HISD improves its outcomes (which, as I'll describe later, it is working hard to do). In fact, Chris told me that if the YES network can maintain the quality and progress it has demonstrated so far, it will operate thirteen schools and produce nine hundred college graduates each year by 2020—double the number of low-income college graduates currently generated by all of HISD each year.

I recently had a chance to visit one of Chris's schools, YES Southwest, in Houston. Founded in 2004, the campus serves six hundred sixth through eleventh graders, virtually all of whom are from low-income households and virtually none of whom have parents who went to college. The school is adding new sixth graders each year and expanding as its oldest cohort of students moves through high school until graduation when, as in all YES Prep schools, every one of them will be expected to apply for, attend, and succeed in college.

Like all YES Prep schools, YES Southwest earned the State of Texas's highest school ranking of "exemplary" based on student performance indicators such as state-assessment passing rates and student dropout rates. More than 95 percent of students at YES Southwest met state proficiency standards across all subject areas— math, reading, English and language arts, social studies, and science. (The percentage of YES students who earned the very highest scores and were "commended" by the state varies from school to school, but in many classes more than half of the students earned that highest honor.)

The motto of YES Prep is "Whatever It Takes." After a tour of the school I had a chance to ask both Chris Barbic and the director of this particular school what that "whatever" actually is. What makes YES Prep Southwest such a successful and special place for students? How is YES Prep different from so many other schools that are not getting these results?

For Chris, there's nothing theoretical about that question. He had spent a couple of years inside a natural laboratory that might have been (but wasn't) purposefully designed to answer it. Chris had opened the fifth YES Prep campus on the third floor of an HISD campus, Robert E. Lee High School. For the several years prior, Lee High School had missed the federal Adequate Yearly Progress benchmarks and, in the year that YES Prep occupied space in the building, was placed on the district's "academically unacceptable" list. That year (2007), a national study published by Johns Hopkins University and the Associated Press put Lee on a list of "dropout factories" where at least 40 percent of freshman do not make it to graduation.[5] After just one year, the students at YES Prep distanced themselves from their peers downstairs. Ninety-six percent of YES Prep sixth graders met grade-level standards in reading, and 95 percent met them in math. (The city averages were 64 percent and 62 percent, respectively.)

Chris answered my question by recalling his daily walk up to the YES Prep school:

> Every time as I headed up to the third floor, I'd peek in at what was happening on the other two floors. It wasn't like all hell was breaking loose—it was more like there was a lot of subtle nothing happening. Kids were working. Teachers were at their desks. But there was no sense of urgency—no "Here's what we're doing today and what it has to do with tomorrow, and here's how it fits in the bigger picture." At best some activities were happening. But it felt like a lot of going through the motions.

And then Chris described what he saw once he made his way to the third floor:

> It just hits you in the face. There's energy. People are flying around. Teachers are working hard at the work of teaching. Kids are excited. And all that is happening because there's a *point* to what's going on. Everything kids are doing ties to something that happened the day before. They know where things are going. There's a long-term goal of college. There's a short-term goal of the unit plan we're working on, and everyone—kids too—knows how the short and the long term fit together. There was a direction, you know? Kids know what the direction was, and adults are guiding them through that. The leadership team is guiding and coaching teachers who are guiding and coaching kids, and we're all rowing in the same direction. They all know why they are there. They all know what the systems are. It's not us against them or "You stay over there and we'll stay over here, and let's not bug each other." It's a team. And there's a sense of mission.

In about ten seconds, Chris captured what is different about transformational schools.

○ ○ ○

UNLIKE JUST A DECADE AGO, today there are many schools like YES Prep that are putting entire campuses of students on track to success in college. There are growing numbers of traditional schools accomplishing this feat, although there are a few high-performing charter networks and independent charter schools that have accounted for the most significant portion of these schools. Perhaps the best known is the Knowledge Is Power Program (KIPP) network of schools, founded by Teach For America alumni Dave Levin and Mike Feinberg (who were at one point roommates with Chris Barbic).

In the wee hours of a morning back in 1993, Dave and Mike both found themselves racked with concern about their students' futures. The two of them spent an entire night brainstorming how to make it easier for committed teachers to put their students on a level playing field. Having put their own students on an entirely different academic trajectory, they wrestled with the limitations of what a single year of heroic teaching could do, given the reality that their students would have to continue to navigate a system that wasn't designed to meet their needs and wasn't built on high expectations for their potential.

They spent the night imagining a different kind of school. They envisioned a school imbued with a culture of achievement where all the parents, students, and teachers were on a mission to ensure that students graduated from college. They envisioned a campus where teachers would not have to go to the dramatic lengths they had found necessary to build an island of achievement, hard work, and teamwork within a larger school that did not have such a culture. They envisioned a school with longer school days, so that teachers wouldn't need to scrape around to find a way to get students dropped off early and picked up late, and a longer school year. They envisioned a school where every class was based on similarly high academic expectations and every teacher was committed to doing his or her part to ensure students graduated from college.

Dave and Mike started the KIPP schools around that vision—Dave began one school in New York, and Mike began one in Houston. Each of them walked door-to-door in their respective communities, sitting down in the living rooms of low-income families, promising that they would do everything they could to ensure their children were prepared to attend and succeed in college. Despite starting with students who had the same academic performance levels as students attending traditional neighborhood schools, their respective schools were—even in their first years—dramatically outperforming other schools in low-income communities.

On the strength of their original vision and results, supported and guided by philanthropists and founders of the Gap stores Don and Doris Fisher with their generosity and insights about replicating excellence, the KIPP Network today includes ninety-nine schools across the country and counting, with an enrollment exceeding 26,000 students, 83 percent of whom are eligible for the federal free and reduced-price meals program. My husband, Richard Barth, has been serving as the KIPP Network's CEO for five years.

KIPP has managed to maintain the sorts of results that Dave and Mike achieved in their original schools, even as the number of KIPP schools has grown. The average KIPP student starts fifth grade at the 34th percentile in reading and the 44th percentile in math, as measured by norm-referenced exams. After three years in KIPP, the same students have moved above the national average; they are performing at the 58th percentile in reading and the 83rd percentile in math. Whereas only 40 percent of the nation's low-income students matriculate to college, 85 percent of KIPP middle school students do so. KIPP high school graduation and college matriculation data appear comparable to those of children from families in the top quartile of income.

As KIPP cofounder Mike Feinberg is known to say, KIPP and other high-achieving networks often encounter a barrage of "yes buts" from skeptics. Some people assume that these schools, even though they are open enrollment, nonetheless "skim" the better students, or kick out the less successful ones, or attract parents with more motivation. A series of rigorous studies have largely put those arguments to rest. The recent Mathematica Policy Research study, for example, found that KIPP schools serve a *larger* proportion of low-income, minority, and low-performing students than the districts at large and that the students coming into KIPP are performing at the same low level as students in the elementary schools that KIPP students attended prior to entry in KIPP. Similarly, the study found no consistent pattern of more or less attrition in KIPP schools relative to non-KIPP schools.[6]

One study, conducted and published by the National Bureau of Economics Research, took a deep and rigorous look at the longitudinal academic progress of kids who won and lost lotteries to get into a KIPP school; it showed dramatic differences in these two groups of students' success.[7] As Mike pointedly asks, "If our success is because we are selecting 'better kids'—an argument that I actually find pretty insulting to kids in low-income communities—then why are the kids selected randomly to be in KIPP doing so much better than those who are not? We have a naturally occurring control group, sadly. If there is no KIPP effect, where are the strong results from kids not accepted by the lottery?"

KIPP and YES Prep are two of the founding examples of success that have helped to inspire dozens of others across the country. Achievement First (in Connecticut and New York City) and Uncommon Schools (in Newark, Boston, New York City, and upstate New York), for example, are inventing similar models with impressive results. In Philadelphia, an organization called Mastery is turning around previously low-performing district schools and dramatically outperforming districtwide averages, producing college-ready graduates. And principals are finding ways of bringing these same strategies into the traditional system, determined to produce transformational, life-changing results within all the rules and regulations of the school district. Across these different schools in different contexts, there are common lessons and patterns we can learn from.

LESSON 1:
SUCCESS IS POSSIBLE EVEN AT THE WHOLE-SCHOOL LEVEL

Until now, we have generally attempted to run schools in urban and rural areas the same way we generally do in high-income communities—giving children learning opportunities and expecting that with a little encouragement, they will make the most of those opportunities. Schools in privileged communities provide children with the opportunities necessary to continue on the trajectory expected of them and predicted by their socioeconomic background. They aren't transformative for the vast majority of their students, simply because they don't need to be. But what we're seeing is that by operating very differently—by enlisting students and their families in a mission to change the outcomes predicted by students' socioeconomic background and giving students the academic experiences and extra supports necessary to accomplish that mission— it is possible to put students in urban and rural areas on a level playing field. In recent years I have made many visits to exceptional schools in underresourced communities, always coming away with a renewed sense of optimism about the impact great schools can have on the educational prospects of our nation's children. On a visit to KIPP Infinity in New York, I was particularly inspired.

Founded by principal Joe Negron and a team of six teachers in 2005, KIPP Infinity today serves almost three hundred low-income fifth through eighth grade students from Washington Heights, West Harlem, and the South Bronx. The incoming fifth graders at KIPP Infinity come in, on average, about one grade level behind in math and between one and a half and two grade levels behind in reading. This is a school that aspires to ensure its students gain the character traits and intellectual skills necessary for success in college and in life. It invests enormous energy to accomplish that end, with students who arrive in fifth grade not only far behind but also experiencing all sorts of extra challenges.

Walking through its halls and sitting in its classrooms is an incredible experience. I met fifth graders walking down the hallway at 7:00 A.M. (and realized that my own fifth grader was at that moment most likely asleep in bed). As I watched Joe (a Teach For America alumnus who serves as the school's principal and also continues to teach) work with his math students to solve a problem, I contemplated the fact that the curriculum at our son's progressive elementary school wasn't as rigorous. I make the comparisons to my own children in an attempt to convey that this is not a school that is simply better than the nearby public schools. This is a school that would be considered academically exceptional by parents with the resources to access the best of what is available. Moreover, in talking with Joe, it became clear just how actively the school supports students and families in its quest to change the outcomes that would typically be expected. For example, beyond the lengthened school day and year that KIPP Infinity provides, KIPP works with parents to ensure students can and do focus on completing two hours of additional homework a night; when that's not possible, the teachers keep students at school to finish it. Determined to ensure its students will succeed in college, KIPP Infinity has what its staff calls a "resiliency curriculum" through which traits like self-confidence, hope, gratitude, grit, and zest are taught, discussed, and tracked. Teachers work together to understand each student's circumstances, strengths, and developmental areas and collaborate to ensure each student has the support, resources, and motivation to succeed. Teachers are available by cell phone 24-7, and the school provides a range of additional health and other services whenever necessary. "We're doing everything from counseling families to procuring coats to writing recommendations for scholarship programs. Our goal is to help the whole child—academics, family, health, and safety included," Joe told me.

KIPP Infinity consistently ranks among the top public schools in New York City. In 2008 it was named the number-one elementary and middle public school in New York City in the Department of Education's annual progress reports—a ranking based on school environment, student performance, student progress, and impact on the achievement gap.[8]

Another particularly inspiring visit was to a school in Newark called North Star Academy Vailsburg Elementary that is run by a Teach For America alumna named Julie Jackson. For years, if not decades, Newark has been held up as a community where the influence of poverty simply could not be overcome with educational interventions. In 2004 Newark was the second-poorest big city in the country, behind Miami. About three-fourths of Julie's students qualify for free and reduced lunch, and virtually all of them are students of color, and she is determined to ensure that her school puts all of them on track to beating the statistical odds.

I vividly recall the urgency and rigor in Julie's math classroom when she was a corps member, and now her school is infused with the same sense of energy around learning that I'd seen in her classroom. I was amazed to see the students' work that was hanging on the wall in this school. I analyzed a wall of kindergarten writing, from each student in both English and Spanish, that far outshined the writing of my kindergartner's class.

Part of a family of three middle schools, another new elementary school, and a high school that is within the broader Uncommon Schools network, North Star Academy Vailsburg Elementary is getting results comparable to those of the best elementary schools in the state, irrespective of its students' socioeconomic status. Though the vast majority of North Star's students show up having had little if any early childhood education, in the school's second year, every single student—virtually all of whom had started below grade level—was scoring at or above grade level on nationally normed assessments of reading, writing, and math skills.

KIPP Infinity and North Star are proving that it is possible to put students on a different trajectory at the whole-school level when we commit ourselves to this end. As we'll see later in the chapter, all of these schools are accomplishing results by adopting a different mission and going to great lengths to execute it. And although these happen to be charter school campuses, we're seeing similar proof of the possibilities on traditional noncharter campuses.

On the same day that I recently visited Chris Barbic's YES Prep campus, I drove across town to Port Houston Elementary. Serving students with roughly the same socioeconomic demographics as YES Southwest, Port Houston Elementary is a traditional district school in HISD serving students who come from the low-income neighborhood in which it sits. Geographically isolated among warehouses storing goods being shipped in and out of the Port of Houston, and lacking in public transportation services, it's a neighborhood that has more than its share of crime and gang activity. A third of its residents are under the age of eighteen, and in 2000 the median household income was $24,006.[9] Virtually all (96 percent) of Port Houston's students qualify for free or reduced lunch. The vast majority are learning English as a second language.

Statistically speaking, these demographics suggest that this school's students are likely to be living representatives of the achievement gap, unable to compete with children in the suburbs who have more support, resources, and advantages. Yet the school's statistics show that the children at Port Houston Elementary are defying the odds in dramatic fashion. They are excelling at levels that rival schools in wealthy neighborhoods.

I spent a couple of hours touring the school, observing classrooms, and talking with students and parents with the school's then principal, Reid Whitaker, a Teach For America alumnus who had led his students to dramatic academic progress, was runner-up for Teacher of the Year in the Houston ISD, and was tapped to lead the school after only three years in the classroom.

I was amazed to see what Reid had done. He had accomplished what I had previously seen only in the most successful charter schools—building an extraordinary culture of achievement, attracting an exceptional faculty, and achieving incredible student results. When I was there I met one of the parents. She used to deliver packages to the school and was so impressed by what she saw there that she found a way to move into the district to be able to send her daughter there.

Before Reid took over the school, it was on the verge of being rated "academically unacceptable" by the state. Two years later Port Houston was labeled "exemplary." In 2008–2009 100 percent of the school's sixth graders demonstrated proficiency on the state reading and math exams.

These schools exist, even in traditional district contexts, and are multiplying across the country. I saw another example in New York at the public open-enrollment school serving about four hundred middle and high school students called the Washington Heights Expeditionary Learning School (WHEELS). This school is a member of a national network of "Expeditionary Learning" schools, an approach that emphasizes project- and team-based learning. WHEELS serves almost exclusively students living near and below the poverty line. Students are assigned to WHEELS based on where they live. In our recent visits to the school we saw several children being enrolled in the school midyear, including a boy with special needs from the Dominican Republic who spoke little English. Yet students at WHEELS are demonstrating mastery of skills and knowledge at levels rivaling schools in much higher-income neighborhoods.

School leader Brett Kimmel (a Teach For America alumnus who first taught in Houston before moving to New York) is a little dismissive of the A his campus received from the New York Department of Education. "Lots of elementary and middle schools get As," he says. But Brett is proud of the fact that the children in his school are at the 85th percentile in terms of academic performance in the entire city. "Many of the schools that are ahead of us," he notes, "are well established and make no bones about being selective at their front door. They are only taking in the kids they want to. We are just four years old and we are taking everyone who shows up, and we're on our way to outperforming those schools." In its second year, only 37 percent of WHEELS' incoming sixth graders were on grade level in English and language arts. By the end of seventh grade, 83 percent of those students were on grade level. As those students end eighth grade, Brett thinks that all of them—100 percent—are on pace to be on grade level in reading and math.

On my visits to the schools headed by Joe, Julie, Reid, and Brett, I looked closely at the student work hanging on the walls, and I watched the rich and rigorous interactions in their classrooms. These schools are attaining levels of success that rival and in some cases exceed those at the schools the most economically privileged people in the country are choosing for their own children. Schools like Port Houston Elementary, WHEELS, KIPP Infinity, and North Star—and there are many more—are proving that schools can change the trajectory of their students.

LESSON 2:
THERE ARE NO SHORTCUTS

I remember visiting Dave's original KIPP Academy in the Bronx years ago and asking him what it really was that accounted for the school's extraordinary success. He looked at me blankly: "It's nothing. It's all the basics." True to the mantra that you see in KIPP schools everywhere, "There Are No Shortcuts," Dave was trying to communicate that there was nothing elusive and nothing magical about the success. These schools' success derives from a commitment to putting students on a different academic trajectory, regardless of what it takes to achieve this goal, and from all the hard work and intentionality involved in building any high-performing enterprise. Just as great teachers operate like successful leaders in other contexts, the strategies successful schools pursue are surprisingly similar to those that are required for success in any organization pursuing ambitious aims.

A Vision for Transformational Change

Joe Negron told me about an incoming fifth grader at KIPP Infinity who cried every day of summer school four years ago because he was unaccustomed to the homework load and the high expectations of his teachers. Now, as a rising ninth grader, that young man is a proud alumnus who ran on the cross country team for three years, played in the concert band, cared for the school pets, and rose from a well-below-grade-level reader to an on-grade-level reader and writer. Without the extra supports, high expectations, and warmth that pervade the school, this young man could easily have been defeated by challenges he has faced growing up. This student's story is reflective of the mission and vision of all of the highly successful schools I have visited. They are committed to a changed reality for their students, built on high expectations for student performance, and they're willing to do whatever it takes to realize that vision.

At WHEELS I could not get through the door of the school before Brett Kimmel had articulated the school's vision of success. His vision is that the children will excel in college, and that vision shapes everything about his school:

> Our mission is to prepare our kids to excel in college. We work backwards from that. Being ready for college informs the whole school curriculum—what we study, how we study it, what study and life skills we emphasize. And when we work backwards from that, we realize that kids have to leave eighth grade ready for a rigorous college-preparatory high school experience. That's a critical mile marker along the way of our planned path to college preparation, and that's where we are this year with the eighth graders. We bust our tails to get them there by the end of the eighth grade because then they can embark on our rigorous high school curriculum as we build out our high school. Every decision is steeped in college preparation methodology and philosophy.

Across New York City in Brooklyn, at Achievement First Brownsville, an elementary school serving students in one of the most crime-ridden neighborhoods of New York, school leader Gina Musumeci also does not accept "catching kids up" as success. She intends to completely close the achievement gap between her students and students in high-income, well-resourced schools—a bar much higher than the state and standardized assessments' measure of "grade level." "State proficiency levels are nowhere near these students' potential. We have to set our sights higher. Our vision is that we are preparing them for the day they graduate from college. We are asking ourselves, 'What knowledge, values, and habits do they need to be ultimately successful in life?' and we're planning backwards from that vision. We are creating a rigorous and loving school around that purpose." Gina's school, in only its second year, is posting dramatic results. Starting with children who come through its doors well below grade level in kindergarten, in the 2009 school year more than 95 percent of children were proficient across the school, and more than 55 percent were more than a year ahead.

The commitment to put children fighting the challenges of poverty on a level playing field comes along with a commitment to provide students with extra supports like more time and school-based social services and health programs in order to get there. These schools build in a longer school day, taking the pressure off teachers to take the initiative to find more time with their kids. At KIPP, for example, schools extend the days, weeks, and academic year to provide students as much as six hundred more hours of school time to catch up and move ahead. Although every KIPP school is a little different, they also build a web of support for children and their families that includes a social worker and doctor. At Reid Whitaker's elementary school in Houston, he realized that his kindergartners were showing up already behind, so he rallied his staff to go out into the neighborhood and find two and three year olds and talk with their families about reading with children and engaging them in practices that would build book and print awareness. In Chris Barbic's YES Prep network of schools, two student-support counselors work to connect children to social services that they or their families need. Chris has partnered with Baylor College of Medicine to provide mental health support and pilot programs focusing on nutrition and exercises. He and his staff work to ensure that children are active and involved in school until the time their family is with them at home.

Schools that transform their students' trajectories aspire not to equality of inputs but rather to equality of outputs. They are aspiring not to ensure their students have access to the same books, or dollars, or hours, but rather that they achieve the same levels of performance and learning and the same life opportunities. That means accessing additional resources and doing whatever it takes to level the playing field for their students.

People, People, People

As I have the opportunity to visit with leaders of one successful school after another, I ask them the obvious question, "Why is your school succeeding?" In almost every case, their first answer is the same: people. "The answer won't surprise you," WHEELS' Brett Kimmel said. "Everything starts with teacher quality. There are many factors at play, but I'm dead in the water if I don't have great teachers. It all comes down to the two-sided coin of teacher recruitment and retention." This priority—find highly effective teachers and keep them—is perhaps the most labor-intensive part of a successful school leader's job. "I spend most of my time," Chris Barbic said, "thinking about how to find, and do we have, and how do we keep, and are we developing, the right people in our schools."

With the search for highly effective teachers at the top of every school leader's list and with the pipeline of highly effective teachers limited, the "talent war" among the growing number of successful schools is intense. "I'll e-mail anybody," Joe Negron told me as we walked around KIPP Infinity. Though Joe is quick to credit his teachers with the school's incredible success, it is also clear that these are teachers he himself has searched for, cajoled, begged, and won over to join him to achieve their vision of success for their students. "Seriously, I'll talk to anybody about working here. Wendy, do you remember Leyla Bravo? She's right there in that room. Phenomenal teacher. I saw her on the news in a classroom where you were being interviewed. I thought, 'She must be really good.' So I e-mailed her. She took some convincing, but she joined us. Remember when Jason Kamras got named Teacher of the Year? I e-mailed him and asked him if we could talk. It's a full-time job to be cultivating talent."

Just as we do in our selection and admissions team at Teach For America, these school leaders obsess over the question of what characteristics predict teachers' success with their students and how to find and hire more of those people. They are coming to the same findings about the importance of personal characteristics and dispositions. Chris Barbic and his colleagues at YES Prep, for example, have used a battery of psychological tests with their teachers, searching for the dispositions of teachers who are getting the best results. YES Prep has learned that certain characteristics, like "rebound time" (the time it takes to get back engaged after a setback), willingness to address conflict, high energy level, and the like are predictive of success in their context, so they are looking for those traits in their new hires.

Interestingly, Chris also discovered in these studies that his most effective teachers are not wild optimists. Instead, they tend a little toward pessimism. "I thought that was strange at first, but it actually makes a lot of sense," he told me. "These are people who don't assume everything is going to turn out okay. They are expecting and taking on inevitable setbacks. They know things don't just work out without hard work."

Joe Negron, at KIPP Infinity, has learned to look for similar characteristics. He says he also looks for the ability to handle tough feedback and turn things around quickly when something fails or is not working—how good someone is at "failing and learning." "I think the biggest key is self-awareness and ownership," Joe says. "Second is a determination to do whatever it takes to get your kids where they need to be. Do you hold up the mirror when things go wrong? Do you embrace responsibility for children's success?" He says that for him, "Every red flag in an interview counts. The key to every teacher's professional growth is being around a lot of great people who are working hard and learning together."

But teacher recruitment is only half the battle. Keeping great teachers is another full-time effort, especially in a context where extraordinary effectiveness is unfortunately still rare. Successful school leaders know that teachers stay when they are surrounded by colleagues and a culture that value their contributions. Successful school leaders also think constantly about how to give their most successful teachers opportunities for broader impact. Virtually all of these schools, for example, have systematized the idea that particularly effective teachers become, in one way or another, "master teachers" who coach and guide colleagues.

Also critically important is a teacher's sense that he or she can and will grow professionally as an instructor and leader. This is an additional motivation—alongside increasing student success—that is driving many of these school leaders to focus so heavily on meaningful and differentiated teacher development in their schools. "The conversation starts with recruitment, identification, and hiring of great teachers," says Brett at WHEELS. "But then it is the support of those teachers along the way that keeps them invested and engaged. The first step is finding great people. The next step is supporting them to go from good to great or from great to greater." Since he began WHEELS, he has lost only a handful of teachers, perhaps two or three per year. His 90 percent retention rate is almost unheard of in many schools in low-income communities.

I don't see such a focus on recruiting and developing great people in less successful schools. On a recent visit to an exceptional teacher's classroom, I was once again inspired by the profound impact a single teacher can have on a group of students' lives. After observing and visiting the teacher, the school's principal came in to say hello. She told me how fantastic this teacher was and how, while the principal generally liked Teach For America, she thought the two-year commitment was simply too short and that we should change that.

The most effective principals I've met do everything they can think of to persuade their teachers to stay—and they are very often successful. I later learned from the teacher I was observing that the school leadership had simply assumed he would leave and had no discussions with him about it. Yet as word of his effectiveness spread, he was recruited by many strong leaders at other schools who were engaging in the fight to find and retain great people.

At Teach For America about 60 percent of our teachers teach a third year. But behind those numbers is a critically important story: There are some campuses where virtually every teacher leaves after their two-year commitment, and others where a very high percentage stay after their two-year commitment. The difference is the school leadership's commitment to developing, supporting, and challenging their staff. "Look, I came into Teach For America thinking I was going to do this for my life," Joe Negron told me. "But I do hire people who say 'I'm thinking about teaching a short time.' If they are great, I'll take them, and then I find ways to make them happy and want to stay." Incredibly, every founding teacher who started at KIPP Infinity six years ago is still at the school—and every single one of them has earned the KIPP Network's prestigious Excellence in Teaching Award.

School leaders in traditional schools often have less power to choose their teachers than leaders in charter schools, yet effective principals find a way to build their dream teams. As I toured Port Houston Elementary with Reid, he was rattling off the awards his teachers had earned: ESL [English as a Second Language] Teacher of the Year, Elementary Teacher of the Year, and on and on. The key, he says, is a strong school culture of achievement that is attractive to the most effective teachers in the city. Ineffective teachers

left, and strong teachers wanted to continue to work in the culture
he was creating:

> If you create a culture of positive goodwill that is built on
> team responsibility and centered on really high expecta-
> tions for students, people who are not team players leave. I
> have worked hard to create a culture that attracts the right
> people and repels the people who should go. I've only fired
> one teacher, but a number of teachers have left because they
> knew they weren't giving their all and didn't want to be in
> the spotlight here. In our school, anyone who is not giving
> 100 percent to tutorials, who is not working as a team mem-
> ber, who is not working so hard for their students, they
> stand out like a sore thumb, and that's uncomfortable.

Indeed, building a strong culture is critical to the success of all the
transformational schools I've visited.

A Culture of Achievement

Sehba Ali, who began her career as a Teach For America corps member in Houston and then founded KIPP Heartwood in California,
drove this point home for me as she described the vision and culture
of her school. I had asked to talk with her because I had heard that
her school, serving students from low-income families in East San
Jose, had become one of the very highest-performing public schools
in California—based on California's standards, it was among the top
3 percent of schools in the state. When Sehba's students first arrived
at her school, they were near the 30th percentile in reading and at
the 50th percentile in math compared with other students across the
country. Just two years later, the school's sixth graders were at the 95th

percentile in math and at the 78th percentile in reading. When the *San Jose Mercury News* rated schools based on sixth grade math scores, her school's students tied for first place as the highest-performing students in math in the entire county, outscoring students in the affluent communities of Palo Alto, Los Gatos, and Los Altos.

One of the first words Sehba used to describe the vision for her school was "community." She sought to build a community of students who have the academic skills and strength of character to be successful in college and to make positive change throughout their lives. She named her school KIPP Heartwood, which is the term for the living tissue of redwood trees. Redwood trees are a symbol of strength in the Bay Area—if something happens to a redwood tree, it rebuilds from the heartwood. She is working to foster the development of students who will be similarly resilient in the face of immense challenges.

From that vision Sehba developed clarity about the culture of the school. Her school, she determined, would exude HEART— honor, excellence, absolute determination, responsibility, and teamwork. She and her team of teachers worked to infuse those values into decisions and conversations. For Sehba, the ideal of HEART is inextricably tied to the ceremony of a teacher, student, and family all signing a contract of collective commitment to work hard to achieve the school's vision. The students commit to work hard, the parents commit to ensure their kids are at school and that they finish their homework, and the teachers commit to do whatever it takes to ensure their students excel.

I often hear people describe a school's culture as something that one can "feel" in a school but not describe, as something that just "happens." As I have observed and learned from successful school leaders, though, I have seen that a successful campuswide culture is intentionally created. Sehba emphasized that the culture at Heartwood is built, not discovered:

We wanted students to ultimately leave the school with great academic achievement, but also as responsible young adults with tenacity and grit. Creating an environment that constantly reinforced those ideas was very deliberate. We have a list of 150 elements of the students' experience—everything from what kids should experience when they arrive to how they throw away garbage to how they get their lunch. Before every school year, we go over that list as an entire staff, asking ourselves what expectations to set that will best reinforce our core values and culture. For example, at KIPP Heartwood, the students sitting at a table together in the cafeteria are expected to not eat until everyone at the table has their food—not only is that learning social norms, but it reinforces our sense of team and that lunch is a time to build community.

I recently talked with a student named Sergio, who entered KIPP Heartwood in fifth grade and is now a junior at the KIPP San Jose Collegiate High School. Sergio said that unlike other KIPP students, he didn't enroll in KIPP to get on track to go to college. "I just did it to go on the field trips," he said. "I didn't really care about school." Sergio said that he spent his first three years misbehaving and failing to meet the school's expectations. But then, in eighth grade, he says he looked at his options in life and saw that college would make life a lot easier. What brought about the change? Sergio says his teachers reinforced the same messages over and over, told him that he had to change and that it was up to him, and surrounded him with love and support. Now, as a high school student, Sergio says he's changed a lot about the way he manages his time and the way he studies, and most of the changes have been on his own. KIPP's culture inspired Sergio to take responsibility for his education. "If it weren't for KIPP I'd be on the streets by now," he told me. "My family could never have supported me in a normal school. Now I'm going to be a first-generation college student."

Culture building gets the same focus and attention in every highly successful school I've visited. "We've been really purposeful—very thoughtful about mapping out the structures, policies, and procedures that generate the school culture," Brett told me about his work at WHEELS. Before the school opened its doors, Brett and the dozen founding faculty cleared an entire day of the summer to talk through school culture. Their method was revealing: They literally went through the entire day in the life of a WHEELS student, minute by minute, from the moment the student opened her eyes in the morning to the moment she went to sleep:

> At every moment, we asked ourselves, what about this moment of the day is or is not fostering college readiness in our students? We realized that what kids have for breakfast matters to learning, so we talked about when and how we were working with students and families to ensure they were getting a good breakfast. These are middle school kids, and this is the first time certain hygiene issues are coming into play. How are we talking to our students about that in a way that ensures they feel good about themselves? Then the kids are getting dressed. What kind of clothes are they putting on? Jeans? A uniform? Every question we put through the filter of college readiness.

Brett says it took his team four or five hours of this envisioning exercise before their imagined student even arrived at school, and then they dug in on a whole range of questions about what the student feels, hears, and sees upon crossing the threshold: "How do they get up to our floor? How are they welcomed? What's the appropriate way to walk in a building, and when and how are we teaching that? I could keep going and going. We literally left no stone unturned. Eventually, we got to the point where students are ready to start class, and we said, 'What does that look like? How is this organized?' We really wanted to simplify school structures and organizations so it demystified for kids what school is about."

Brett insists that this level of attention is what a great school culture requires: going through every second of the day and asking what adults could and should do to align with their mission and vision of preparing kids to attend college. The culture is proactively created with hard, purposeful work. It is the intense attention to aligning the details of student experiences, norms, and interactions with the vision of the school. Chris Barbic at YES Prep put it this way:

> It'd be easy for people to say, "Now that we've opened up seven schools, the culture is going to take care of itself because everyone knows what to do." But it doesn't work that way. You've got to be intentional about it. You've got to have a detailed game plan for the culture you want. And it's everything from how are kids going to enter the classroom, how are they going to walk onto campus, how are they going to sit down, how are you going to run a morning meeting, how are transitions going to work—thinking through every system and being sure they are tight and everyone is on board and the kids get them. I think it starts with that.

Managing High-Performing Teams

Successful school leaders are all obsessed with, as Chris says, ensuring the team is "rowing in the same direction." Everyone, North Star's Julie Jackson says, needs to be "ready and prepared to play in the big game" of working hard to fulfill their vision of college readiness. Reid says everyone needs to "share a common view of the future and want to contribute to getting there."

Chris is working to build a fully aligned team that is working together and assuming collective responsibility for success:

> This isn't just about getting great teachers and putting them in the classroom. What we are really trying to do is create a band. The band has to work together. You have to have a team. At some schools, the teachers go in the room and shut the door and block out all the dysfunction outside the classroom. Interaction with anyone else in the building is avoided at all costs. Here it is the exact opposite. We all own whatever dysfunction is outside the door, together. We are working together for our kids. That's part of our school culture, and you cannot work here and not love that.

Accomplishing this requires very effective management. "I used to think 'management' was a dirty word," Joe Negron said. "I've learned from other school leaders in and around KIPP just how critically important and powerful good management is to creating the experiences we want for our children."

At KIPP Infinity, every teacher has a weekly "one-on-one" with a manager (either Joe, an instructional leader, or a dean) at a dedicated time, during which teachers review areas where they need more support and managers discuss the teacher's progress toward various performance goals. "We know whether these one-on-ones are being used well if, at the time of a performance review, there are no surprises," Joe says. "Where this team member is, whether good progress is being made, what the teacher needs in terms of support and coaching—all of those issues have to be on the table at least once a week and hopefully more often than that."

Joe emphasizes that the critical purposes served by these management structures go well beyond improving teachers' effectiveness. "It doesn't sound that revolutionary to have one-on-ones with every teacher every week, but it's absolutely critical. This is the venue for people's voices to be heard, for problem solving, for being sure that everyone is getting what they need to do their job."

The fact that these school leaders are thinking so deliberately about management at all distinguishes them from many conventional incarnations of the principal role. In many schools one principal is technically the manager of fifty or even one hundred teachers, and there may be little, if any, interaction—not to mention effective management—happening in that relationship. "When I was teaching, I met with my principal only once. I never met with any sort of coach," Joe recalls. "That system just cannot get us where we need to be. I do understand why that happens. There are always twenty things tugging at a school leader. The day can become very reactive, but if you want to create an exceptional school, you have to set aside time in the calendar to hear from, coach, and manage your team members."

Having clearly defined goals and measures of success is a foundational requirement for building aligned teams and managing them well. "True alignment takes clear measures," Achievement First's Gina Musumeci says. "We have to know what success is in college, but we also have to know what all the little benchmarks along the way are. That takes a lot of planning and a lot of attention to what students are learning. I need to know what I want them to know and do in fourth grade, so that helps me know what I want from them in kindergarten. And those measures help me know how to support and push my team members."

Gina and her team, in an exercise that is replicated across the Achievement First network of campuses, translate their ambitious vision of student success into clear measures that drive their daily actions. For example, at Achievement First Brownsville, the goal is not only that 100 percent of students in third grade will be performing at least on grade level in literacy and math, but that more than 60 percent will score at the advanced level. Gina also is evolving methods of assessing goals for student values and habits alongside the academic ones. She and her team track, for example, attendance, homework completion, and anonymous surveys of children asking about instances of unsolicited kindness by their peers.

I see this same emphasis on transparency of progress, in the form of rigorous and meaningful student-performance data, in all of these highly successful schools. Reid Whitaker, at Port Houston, unabashedly gushed about his love for meaningful data on his students' progress, precisely because it helps increase student learning:

> I believe in the data—I believe in its impact on kids' lives. When I first suggested that as a school we commit to weekly progress assessments, some teachers were taken aback. They said, "But that's going to take away instructional time." But I assured our team that if we do this right, the data from those weekly assessments will be so valuable for instruction. If we don't know each week what kids have and have not understood, then so much of our instructional time is wasted. We simply have to know whether a student got this concept or did not get this objective. Now, today, our whole team is so into it. I think everyone sees the value of those weekly assessments to their instruction, and the teachers, not me, run the whole system.

Many educators and parents across the nation are frustrated by one aspect or another of utilizing academic assessments. These leaders are too, but they want to see deeper, more rigorous, and more thorough assessments—not fewer of them. In their experience, the problem with standardized assessments is their quality, not their existence.

These school leaders are relying on the student data, but they are also doing everything they can to understand whether their schools are accomplishing their missions. They are in and out of classrooms frequently to understand how their teachers and students are doing. "Julie Jackson is not spending her days the way most principals typically do—sitting in the office on the phone dealing with petty, bureaucratic concerns," Norman Atkins, one of the founders of the Uncommon Schools network of which North Star is a part, told me. "She's peripatetic, constantly in classrooms, looking at instruction, supporting teachers, and giving feedback on lesson plans."

As I have walked through these schools and in and out of classrooms with Julie, Reid, Brett, Gina, and others, it has been clear that everyone—teachers and students alike—expects those visits. These school leaders are present in the school experience as they seek to complement the student achievement data and other measures they are analyzing with what they can see and learn from teachers and students themselves—all in the spirit of ensuring that every teacher is leading students to fulfill their potential.

Like all of these school leaders, Gina sets a high bar for teacher effectiveness and, along with a small team of teacher coaches, is always evaluating her team members' progress—both with the data coming in from the classrooms and through her observations and interactions with her team members—to ensure that everyone is meeting those standards. One of the warmest and kindest people I've ever met, she pulls no punches when it comes to ensuring her students are getting what they deserve:

> We are adults. We are going to be fine. These children are
> extremely vulnerable, and we've made promises to them and

their parents. *Anything* that gets in the way of that must be taken out of the equation. I do believe coaching is very valuable, but ultimately if you don't see children progressing or the teacher progressing, then it is not a good fit and the adult needs to go somewhere else. This is not the right fit for everyone. People have to know—and our team does know—that I am warm and that I love them, I truly do love them, so when I do have to say, "This isn't working, you can't continue, I don't think this is the best place for you," I don't think they think I'm harsh or unreasonable. They know I am going to do whatever our kids need to be done.

For Gina, those difficult conversations with team members whom she has to move out of the school community loop right back to the first priority common to all of these highly effective school leaders: finding and keeping great talent. "The only way for me to maintain my highest-performing teachers is to be sure they understand that mediocrity is not tolerated," she says. "It is hard to work your tail off when others aren't. When they see that the bar is high for everyone, that inspires them and makes them invested."

○ ○ ○

MUCH LIKE THE SUCCESSFUL TEACHERS we got to know in the previous chapter, these schools are showing us what it takes to achieve transformational results, and the keys to success are strikingly consistent at the classroom and school levels.

Successful teachers and school leaders all have visions for changing the educational trajectory of their students. They all create powerful cultures of achievement, wherein students and families take responsibility for their own educations. They all embrace the hard work of effective execution and all that entails in their respective realms. They all do whatever it takes to achieve success, going far above and beyond traditional expectations for what classrooms and schools should be. Together, they show us that there's nothing elusive about putting urban and rural students on a different trajectory. Unfortunately, it's a lot of hard work, and fostering the development of thousands of high-performing schools will be challenging.

LESSON 3:
REPLICATING SUCCESS WILL TAKE DEVELOPING AND UNLEASHING LEADERSHIP (AND TIME)

Today there is widespread acknowledgment that it is possible to build schools that attain transformational results and replicate them. The challenge now is to scale this success—to create hundreds and ultimately thousands of successful schools. What will it take?

While I will save the question of how to create whole school districts of excellent schools for the next chapter, here it seems most instructive to understand what the managers of the charter school networks that have produced so many of the lighthouse schools would say to this question. I asked Norman Atkins, given his experience at Uncommon Schools, which currently has twenty-four schools and is working to expand to thirty-eight in the next five years; my husband, Richard Barth; KIPP's cofounder Mike Feinberg; and Dacia Toll, co–chief executive of Achievement First, which currently has nineteen schools and is working to grow to thirty in the next five years.

First, they each responded, it takes a robust people pipeline. "Great teaching and more of it," says Mike, one of the key thinkers behind KIPP's successful expansion to dozens of schools. "Everything we do has to drive to that idea."

Beyond the central importance of finding a path to more and more excellent teachers, replicating one model school to create dozens requires developing a pipeline of extraordinary school leaders. Indeed, perhaps the most striking fact about all of these highly successful schools is the caliber and passion of their leaders. It takes time to find and develop such leaders, who must have certain foundational experiences—namely, the experience of transformational teaching. The leaders of dramatically successful schools are almost always driven by their own extraordinary success with low-income students in their own classrooms. As a result, they have an unshakable belief in the potential of children, they have a very real understanding of what it takes to change the trajectory of students growing up in poverty, and they bring to the challenge the moral authority and credibility to lead a faculty of others to audacious goals. Building successful schools requires, first and foremost, a pipeline of exceptionally successful teachers who themselves have school leadership potential. "The issues of teacher and leader supply are two sides of the same problem," Norman said. "If we increased the supply of teachers who have the mindset and skills that Teach For America and no-excuses schools teach, those folks would go on to become the deans and the principals and the professors in the system."

Dacia Toll says that she thinks about the enablers of growth at Achievement First as being four things: people, culture, systems, and politics. But she thinks she can plan for culture and for the systems necessary to grow her network of schools through thinking deliberately and planning intentionally. And she believes there have been sweeping changes in the political landscape that have made it easier to gain the funding and facilities to open new schools. The thorniest dilemma is developing an effective leadership pipeline. "This takes time," she says. "This is the thing we haven't been able to accelerate."

KIPP, Uncommon Schools, and Achievement First have teamed together to create Teacher U, a program that Norman now runs in collaboration with Hunter College that trains teachers for their schools in New York City. Moreover, each of the networks has made a serious investment in recruiting and developing their teachers and leaders.

Another related and central dilemma that each of these charter system leaders grapples with is how to ensure quality even as the number of schools grows. "When we first started," Norman says, "we thought, 'Let's hire great teachers and good things will happen.' When your school serves 100 kids, that works. When your network has thirty-eight schools and an enrollment goal of 15,000 kids in five cities, you need a new strategy."

Uncommon Schools has invested in training its teachers in common techniques so that there is a shared language across the network. "One of the best things we do as a network is inspect each other's schools. The improvement plans that come out of those visits are very rich," he says, "since people are heading for the same goals and have the same vocabulary."

KIPP has spent a good deal of time grappling with the question of how to maintain a culture of innovation and entrepreneurship—elements clearly present in successful single schools—even while scaling. Achieving this has meant being clear about what is nonnegotiable and where leaders have total freedom. Every KIPP school shares the same mission, which is preparing students for success in college and in life. There is total central control over the indicators used to track progress against that mission, such as college matriculation and completion of eighth grade, student attrition, and teacher retention. Other nonnegotiables include more time and the requirement that every adult who works at KIPP chooses to be there. At the same time, KIPP leaves the choice of curriculum, for example, and its choice of school values up to its individual school leaders. All hiring and financial resource allocations are also owned within each local school.

Maintaining this balance of what is centralized and what is not is what enables the kind of innovation taking place at KIPP Infinity to flourish. If KIPP had dictated one approach to teaching middle school English language arts, Joe and his teachers would not have been at liberty to create their now heralded nonfiction studies program that has resulted in academic gains in reading that are double those of other high-performing KIPP schools. Richard explains that when you attract the right kind of people, who are aligned around the mission and committed to transparency, the central organization does not need to dictate how teachers and leaders approach their semester, months, and days, and when something works it spreads without any central mandate. He also believes this is key to attracting and keeping outstanding talent over time.

Dacia describes Achievement First's evolution toward becoming more flexible. What has driven the change? "First, we love outcomes, and we discovered that if you're focused on inputs as opposed to outcomes, it leads to bad outcomes. Second, most talented people want the autonomy to do what they think is in the interest of kids. Third is a practical challenge—the larger you get, the harder it is to manage tightly," she said. "Overall, we stepped back and realized that when we were founded, our success was a function of an entrepreneurial, whatever-it-takes, performance-oriented approach. What we know about successful schools is that there's a strong sense of ownership at the school site, and we want to foster that sense—that student outcomes are primarily within the school team's control." These charter management organizations would be the first to say that they have long roads and steep learning curves in front of them as they grow, yet they provide a grounded and useful perspective to inform our efforts to scale success.

CONCLUSION

As I was working on this book, I had the opportunity to visit one of the Mastery schools in Philadelphia. The Mastery Network is one of the forces behind the recent proliferation of schools that are attaining transformational results in that city. I visited the Shoemaker campus—a school that in 2006 had been a failing institution, with 16 percent of seventh graders proficient in math and 20 percent in reading.[10] The Mastery Network, a charter management group that specializes in "turning around" failed schools, came in and took over the campus. The school was repainted and small structural changes were made in the building's design, but, more important, Mastery brought to the campus the same lessons we are learning from all the most successful schools across the country.

One of Mastery's students—a young woman from the neighborhood around the school who had been a student on the campus before Mastery took over—gave me a tour. "We used to come to school to have fun and hang out," she said, describing the campus before the Mastery Network's founder, Scott Gordon, and his team took over. "Kids would come to school and get searched, and there were lots of fights. Now it is completely different—there are roles and responsibilities for us, there's more discipline, and the ways teachers teach—they really care if we get it."

Mastery recruited a new principal and a new staff of teachers (about 30 percent are Teach For America corps members or alumni) and also built a network of support services into the school.

On every measure, Mastery's students are dramatically outperforming student averages across the district. After Mastery assumed management of its schools, without a change in the student population, test scores increased an average of 52 percentage points per subject in every grade, while violence dropped 80 percent and student retention increased dramatically. Mastery schools have actually closed the achievement gap in eighth grade math, and two campuses have closed the achievement gap in reading. In 2009, 100 percent of the graduating class was accepted to college. Mastery students have received over $2 million in scholarships.[11]

At Shoemaker I had the chance to talk to Scott, who began his career in the corporate world at General Foods, left that work to train high school dropouts to become nurses' aides, and got to know a number of children in Philadelphia's low-income neighborhoods through his work. He saw that children with incredible potential started to fall behind and drop out as they reached adolescence. After one of the children he was close to was shot and paralyzed, he quit his job and started Mastery. Building successful schools is "all about building functional high-performing organizations," he told me.

Scott Gordon is an understated, even-keeled, and intensely humble person. The point in our conversation where he got most excited and emotional was talking about the need for good and efficient systems in schools. "I don't get it," he said. "Why are so many schools not focusing on talent development, great management, and clear goals? It's not just a nonprofit thing because the best hospitals do this well. It's just an education thing—we have such a hard time doing what we know works."

Mastery is changing the prospects for children in Philadelphia because of its mission and its commitment to do whatever it takes, and because of its focus on all the basics that it takes to build any high-performing organization. "It's all so basic," Joe Negron says of what has made Infinity one of the best schools in New York City. "It really is basic."

Scaling up these successes is incredibly difficult, but we can no longer claim that the obstacle to success is know-how. Successful school leaders across the country are showing us what works.

3

SCALING SUCCESS
LESSONS FROM IMPROVING SYSTEMS

W E DO NOT—YET—HAVE EVIDENCE of undeniable success in ensuring strong educational outcomes across whole communities. However, in a number of cities where racial and economic achievement gaps seemed most intractable just five years ago, today we are seeing historic progress and improvement. New York City, New Orleans, and Washington, D.C., for example, offer immense hope for the future both in their solid progress on reliable measures of student achievement and because their examples reveal patterns that are not only similar to each other but consistent with the patterns we've seen in successful urban and rural classrooms and schools. The pace of change and the progress I see in these and other communities give me great confidence that we will soon be talking about whole school districts that offer proof that success is possible, just as we now have at the classroom and school levels.

I can remember the exact moment that sparked my own confidence that success could be possible, even across an entire system of schools. It was in 2003 when New York City's mayor, Michael Bloomberg, and his appointed chancellor of schools, Joel Klein, outlined their plans to bring principles of management and accountability to the New York City school system. The moment was memorable for me because, although such principles have long been the bedrock on which success is built in most other sectors of society, they weren't something people in education circles generally viewed as the levers for reform back then. With refreshing candor and clarity, the mayor and chancellor accepted responsibility for students' failure and success and set a clear and ambitious vision of a system that would actually produce transformational outcomes. They indicated in their speeches and policies that they were going to bring to New York City schools the same principles of effective organization building that have proved important for any institution—a heavy emphasis on finding, supporting, and keeping great people and clear lines of accountability, management, and support for every role at every level. I remember the shock and anticipation I felt listening to the leaders of this massive school system embrace the principles that we know actually work.

In the years since setting out that bold new approach, New York City has proved to be a model of the fortitude and patience necessary for sustained change. New York is the system that has made the longest commitment to the kinds of reforms we are now seeing elsewhere, and despite the scale of the New York City system— 1,600 schools, 80,000 teachers, 1.1 million students[1]—the needle is moving against the achievement gap in ways that are meaningful for students. While today many people point to the rapid and sometimes rocky changes happening in places like Washington, D.C., and New Orleans as the frontier of districtwide reform, New York City provided the road map that is inspiring much of the change we see around the country. While Joel Klein has resigned as chancellor, his legacy is one of profound progress.

From the start chancellor Joel Klein made an unprecedented investment in human capital. Within a year of taking office, he raised $75 million in private philanthropy[2] to create the Leadership Academy, designed to train and develop a new generation of principals. He also made an unprecedented investment in teacher recruitment to close the teacher-qualification gap between schools in low-income and high-income parts of the city; much of this strategy involved expanding the Teaching Fellows program, which the New Teacher Project helped establish to recruit talented professionals to transition into the classroom, and bringing in substantial numbers of Teach For America corps members. At the same time, the chancellor overhauled his senior team and the staff of his central office.

A few years into his tenure, Joel reorganized the system to inspire the kind of innovation and entrepreneurship that, as we saw in the previous chapter, is important for proliferating transformational schools. With a variety of initiatives, he focused on creating more diverse options for parents and students. "I'm not a charter guy or a traditional guy but a schools guy," he told me. He embraced charters and did everything he could to encourage their growth in New York, and he also embraced the breakup of large failing schools into a new generation of small schools within the public system. For the traditional schools, he pushed responsibility for budgeting and hiring to the school level to the extent possible. He implemented a new system to capture data on student performance and make it available to educators at every level of the system. Now schools within the system have accountability for results and select from a number of resource centers to support their success. In several regions parents can choose their public schools.

Many of these initiatives have been controversial, not every new school is successful or new principal masterful, and the rapid organizational changes have at times created confusion among parents and teachers. Still, New York City is exhibiting the meaningful and sustained reform that we need in other districts and that we are seeing in a couple of places that we'll explore below.

According to the National Assessment of Educational Progress (NAEP)—a well-respected and internationally normed measure of student learning—New York City's students are making real progress. Ten points on the NAEP equates to roughly a year's worth of learning—and between 2003 and 2009, New York City students were up eleven points in fourth grade math and seven points in eighth grade math; between 2002 and 2009, fourth grade reading scores were up by eleven points as well.[3] In fact, in fourth grade math and reading, New York City now performs at roughly the same level as the nation overall.

In sharp contrast, the rest of New York State has been essentially flat on the NAEP over the same period. New York City's accomplishment is all the more notable given that its students, by comparison, are significantly poorer. A review of New York state assessments reveals a similar picture. An analysis of results from 2002 through 2010 shows that each of the five boroughs comprising New York City made greater gains in math and English scores than any of the state's fifty-seven other counties.[4] Since 2002 the gap in average scores between the city and state closed by 65 percent.

New York City's graduation rate has also gone up significantly. According to data published by the State of New York, from 2005 to 2009 New York City increased its four-year graduation rate from 47 percent to 59 percent (a figure that rises further, to 63 percent, when including August graduates), while the state's next four largest cities went from 47 percent to 49 percent and New York State overall went from 78 percent to 80 percent.[5]

With their steady progress, New York City's leaders laid the groundwork for the seismic shifts happening in districts across the nation. New Orleans and Washington, D.C., provide two additional dramatic examples of systems that are showing considerable improvement in the quest to put entire communities of students in low-income communities on a trajectory that broadens their educational and life opportunities.

LESSON 1:
DRAMATIC POSITIVE CHANGE IS
POSSIBLE, EVEN AT THE SYSTEM LEVEL

NYC Fourth Graders Improve Reading Scores
— *Wall Street Journal online*, May 20, 2010

Report: D.C. Schools Make Most Significant Reading Gains Among Urban Systems
— *Washington Post*, May 21, 2010

LEAP Scores Released Today Show
Marked Improvement for New Orleans Public Schools
— *New Orleans Times-Picayune*, May 20, 2009

Before Hurricane Katrina, decades of educational failure in New Orleans had created a community of adults without basic skills. According to one study, in pre-Katrina New Orleans, 40 percent of adults were unable to read on a sixth grade level.[6] In 2005 fewer than 40 percent of New Orleans high school students taking the Graduate Exit Exam—a not very rigorous test of academic skills and knowledge—demonstrated proficiency in the core academic subjects. For many (or most) students in open-enrollment high schools, the chances of attending—let alone succeeding in—college were virtually zero. As in many low-income communities across the country, only one in ten of the children who were ninth graders in 1994 in New Orleans Public Schools had graduated from college six years after their high school graduation—a number that includes students from the city's selective-admissions high schools.[7] In a singularly painful indicator of the system's failure, the *valedictorian* of one its high schools—a student who had just received an A in Algebra II— failed the math portion of the state's Graduate Exit Exam five times.[8] "This story puts a face on the squandered opportunities, the way we're robbing children of an education," business, community, and state board of education leader Leslie Jacobs told the local paper. "This school had no expectations for this student."[9] As a prominent and influential truth teller and agitator on behalf New Orleans's children—and as the behind-the-curtain architect of the reform structures built before Katrina that accelerated progress after the storm—Leslie was sounding the alarm and plotting an educational revolution well before Katrina.

But even as Leslie was putting structures in place to change the schools, the community had little hope that the situation could change. We had placed corps members there since our inception, and the only change we and the broader community knew we could count on was a virtually annual turnover of superintendent.

Hope was similarly elusive a thousand miles away in Washington, D.C., where for decades the public schools presented a tragic irony. In our nation's capital, in the shadows of massive monuments to our most cherished ideals of freedom and equality, hundreds of thousands of children have been denied the opportunities that arise from an excellent education.

In 2007 D.C. was last in a ranking of all states plus the District of Columbia in reading and math scores for fourth and eighth graders.[10] In 2007 only 8 percent of eighth graders were on grade level in math.[11] What's more, the District exhibited the largest performance gap in the nation between white and black students in the fourth grade. On the secondary level, there was a 70 percent racial gap in some subjects.[12] According to *Education Week*'s annual ratings, the dropout rate in D.C. was more than 50 percent in 2005–

2006.[13] D.C. was near the top of the list in one respect: dollars spent per student.[14] In Washington, D.C., per-pupil expenditures had rocketed to more than 150 percent of the national average.

I remember working to help our D.C. team raise funds for Teach For America's efforts and meeting the city's most civic-minded leaders, who were so disillusioned by years of philanthropic investment that hadn't changed anything that they were simply unwilling to do more. Many had given up on the possibility that student outcomes in the school system could change in any meaningful way.

Several years ago, however, both D.C. and New Orleans experienced tectonic shifts in school governance that accelerated and enabled efforts to improve student outcomes. In D.C., Mayor Adrian Fenty made fixing the schools his central issue and obtained approval from the city council to take control of the schools from the school board. He appointed Michelle Rhee as chancellor, gave her full authority to do what was necessary to fix the system, and pledged to handle the inevitable and difficult political battles that accompany dramatic change. Reflecting on the state of affairs described above, Michelle said as she took the reins in 2007, "To respond to these numbers with anything but radical change to reverse them is an insult to the dignity, potential, and creativity of our children."[15]

I had worked with Michelle in various capacities over the years and knew what kind of transformational leader she was. As a Teach For America corps member in Baltimore in 1992, Michelle led her students to dramatic academic gains. This experience engendered in her a rock-solid conviction about the enormous potential of children in urban areas, a conviction that quickly became apparent as she launched a push to reconstitute a school system to give kids the opportunities they deserve.

After her teaching experience Michelle led the New Teacher Project, initially a spin-off of Teach For America that was designed to help change the way districts and states recruit and train new teachers. As the New Teacher Project's entrepreneurial leader, Michelle expanded the organization into an influential engine of national educational reform, along the way accumulating deep insights about how school districts should work.

In the weeks before this book went to press, Mayor Fenty lost the Democratic primary, which led to Michelle's resignation. She was succeeded by another Teach For America alumna, Kaya Henderson, as interim chancellor. While it is too early to predict the sustainability of the reforms Michelle, Kaya, and their team have put in place, the approach and progress in D.C. over the past few years offer rich insight into what it takes to improve a whole system.

In New Orleans the school governance shifts were enabled by events that were shocking and tragic. After Hurricane Katrina, with more than 100 school buildings damaged or destroyed, and with the district's school board announcing that schools would not reopen for the rest of the year, the state stepped in, moving 102 of the city's worst-performing schools away from the school board's control and into the Recovery School District—a special school district the state had created before the storm to turn around underperforming schools. Since then, the RSD has been closing, consolidating, shifting, and opening schools as facilities and student populations recover, creating a new system that is dramatically different from the one washed away by Katrina.

Today, just a few years after the school systems in D.C. and New Orleans came under new leadership, both districts have undergone dramatic transformation and are demonstrating rapid positive growth on virtually all key indicators of system efficacy—starting with student learning.

Both cities are seeing, for example, unprecedented student progress on the National Assessment of Educational Progress. Over the past few years, D.C. fourth graders' proficiency levels in math increased more quickly than in any other large urban district studied.[16] Other measures of student learning reflect similar trends. Over the past three years—from 2007 to 2010—rising test scores reflected material gains in all tested grades and subjects. In 2007 the D.C. Comprehensive Assessment System (DC CAS) indicated that 29 percent of elementary students were proficient in math and 38 percent in English. By 2010 the scores had improved to 43 percent and 44 percent, respectively. Likewise, on the secondary level, the DC CAS recorded two-year gains of about 14 percent in reading and 17 percent in math.[17] For the first time in thirty years, student attendance in D.C. Public Schools (DCPS) has actually increased; in the previous decade the district had lost more than 39 percent of its student population to the growing number of charter schools in the area.[18]

Meanwhile, in New Orleans, on several of the campuses taken over by the Recovery School District, the growth in the percentage of fourth graders scoring basic or above on state English and language arts assessments has exceeded the statewide growth rate at least tenfold. In math the improvements are even more dramatic.[19] Similar results are evidenced by older students. Two-thirds of the campuses serving eighth graders saw improvements between three and six times the state average in English language arts. In math the improvements for eighth graders are as much as eleven times the average improvements statewide.

The Recovery School District is now the leading school district in the state in terms of increasing the percentage of students scoring basic and above, both for the 2009–2010 academic year and in terms of cumulative gains over the past three years.[20] "Of course, being better than other schools' averages in Louisiana is not saying much, but these schools used to be below the average," state superintendent Paul Pastorek told me with a smile. "And we're not talking about two or three schools. We're talking about forty schools that are improving dramatically. I don't think anyone is really paying attention to it, but damn—it's pretty interesting."

Interesting it is. New Orleans and D.C., both long the poster children for the impossibility of change in education, are now among the fastest-improving districts in the country. These systems' progress means that we must acknowledge that success at the system level may actually be possible—even in places where many have long since given up.

Like New York City's school system, neither New Orleans's nor D.C.'s system is where its leaders want it to be, and given the tumultuous political landscape in all of these places, it is still too early to know whether the pace of change can continue. Yet we simply must acknowledge that there is hope for children even in communities that believe they have the most entrenched of circumstances. For many, this is a revelation in and of itself.

LESSON 2:
WE KNOW WHAT PROGRESS REQUIRES:
A COMMITMENT TO THE BASICS OF
BUILDING HIGH-PERFORMING ORGANIZATIONS

The reforms in D.C. and New Orleans are in some ways quite different from each other. Michelle Rhee brought to D.C. a centrally driven system of management and support of principals and teachers. In the D.C. model, principals and teachers across the district have a clear sense of what methods and outcomes are expected of them, and they are closely managed and supported to implement and achieve these goals. Meanwhile, the New Orleans system, emphasizing individual school leaders' ability to innovate and lead as they see fit while at the same time holding those leaders responsible for meeting clear outcomes, is being built with very little management and support for principals and teachers from a central office.

Though we cannot predict how these models will evolve, and it is also too early to claim victory in any of the systems that are showing signs of progress, we can draw guidance from the fact that for all their differences, as in New York City, the New Orleans and D.C. reforms are working from a core set of common principles. These districts, in different ways, are pursuing the same basic elements that have been proved to drive success in any organization: a clear vision for change that is transformational for students, a strong culture of achievement and accountability, and a heavy focus on finding, selecting, supporting, and retaining great people at every level of the system.

A Vision of a Changed Reality for Students

Paul Pastorek is one of the key architects of the New Orleans reforms. A lawyer, former NASA administrator, and long-term education reformer, he was drafted for the state superintendent of schools position not long after Katrina. Paul's aim is not simply to "fix" New Orleans's broken system. He envisions much more than that. He sees a future where New Orleans is the school district that all others want to emulate. He believes that New Orleans can and will develop a "world-class education system."

I recently met Paul for one of New Orleans's famous meals in a restaurant that actually overlooked his father's headstone. My guess is that his long family history in the rough-and-tumble world of Louisiana business and politics fuels both his ambition for the state's schools and his willingness to ruffle some feathers in pursuit of that vision. (One local journalist noted that Paul is "impatient . . . , loathes mediocrity, hates failure, and pushes sweeping and inherently controversial reforms down a fast track.")[21]

Success in New Orleans, he insists, will be defined not by getting off the bottom of national lists but by ensuring that "every kid in this city is going to get a top-notch education and have all the opportunities and choices that come with that." Paul Pastorek is charging hard to reach this goal. One of his first moves was to hire Paul Vallas, a high-profile partner who shared his vision. I had encountered Paul's intensity and breakneck pace firsthand when he served as superintendent in Chicago and then Philadelphia before moving to New Orleans to head the Recovery School District. Paul Pastorek is a cerebral strategist, while Paul Vallas, an action-oriented man with boundless energy, is the implementer of those ideas on the ground. This "odd couple at the top of the New Orleans school system"[22] is united by a burning conviction that New Orleans will be a beacon on the hill for educational excellence for all children.

Whereas the two Pauls' vision in New Orleans means building something new on a foundation that was literally and figuratively wiped clean by Katrina, Michelle faced a "turnaround" project in D.C. Few leaders would have shared her vision of creating a world-class education system given the profound dysfunction that was the reality in the D.C. schools.

When she arrived, Michelle found 5 million unfiled personnel records stacked up in storerooms,[23] and she discovered that some teachers were not being paid on time while others who had left the system were still receiving paychecks. Twenty-five thousand outstanding work orders for school maintenance sat in the central office.[24] About half the city's schools had not received textbooks by the start of the school year, or received the wrong ones.[25] A D.C. Appleseed report shows that before Michelle arrived, D.C. (with its special education enrollment of more than 11,000) had more pending special education due process hearings open than the entire state of California (with its special education enrollment of more than 600,000)—more than 3,000 hearings were in the backlog.[26] As one education journal described it, D.C. was a "school system that has defied management for decades: that hasn't kept records, patched windows, met budgets, delivered books, returned phone calls, followed court orders, checked teachers' credentials, or, for years on end, opened school on schedule in the fall."[27]

These realities were a fundamental barrier to building a school system that levels the playing field for D.C.'s children. So, for Michelle and her team, the first order of business was to implement and fix the most rudimentary systems necessary for the district to function at all—"brush clearing," they called it. Personnel files had to be cleaned up and updated. E-mail systems had to be introduced so that teachers and administrators could actually communicate. Financial records had to be audited and digitized. And giant streams of inefficiently allocated resources had to be redirected. Defying all naysayers who advised closing down no more than two schools in any given year, Michelle and her team closed down twenty-three schools in the first year based on the fact that some schools were dramatically underenrolled,[28] a move that freed up millions of dollars to ensure that every school in the district actually had an art teacher, a PE teacher, and a nurse.

The essential building blocks of the system were so distressed and decayed that the ultimate vision—that of an efficient team of adults ensuring all students succeed—could have been lost in the haze. But Michelle insisted that the D.C. schools would be the very epitome of our most fundamental ideals. "Our public schools will ensure that every child, regardless of their life circumstances, can achieve at the highest levels and live the American dream if they work hard and do the right thing," she said.

Joel Klein, Paul Pastorek, Paul Vallas, and Michelle Rhee have held high expectations for the students and adults in their systems and have made it clear to everyone in their systems that a commitment to ensuring high levels of student achievement should drive decision making. With their ambitious visions, these leaders have created a sense of purpose and urgency that is striking to those of us who have spent time in these systems for years.

A Culture of Achievement and Accountability

Driven by their similar visions of excellence, these leaders embarked on a quest to create a culture of achievement and accountability for student outcomes. They have insisted that every person in the system understand his or her responsibility for students' success or failure. We must change the system, Michelle said, "so that it is no longer about the needs and preferences of adults, but rather about what we owe our kids."

In Washington, D.C., a few weeks after assuming her role as schools chancellor, Michelle went out to each of the schools in the district to meet with the principals and talk through their goals for the year. She wanted to be sure that every principal had committed to making clear and measurable progress by the end of the year, to hold each principal accountable for those goals, and to hear from principals what support they needed to achieve their goals. This was perhaps an obvious instinct from someone who understands the central role of clear goals and good management. It was, however, the first time many of the principals had ever had discussions like this with any manager.

I had the chance to sit down with three members of Michelle's senior team three years into their effort. Kaya Henderson (the recently announced interim chancellor) had taught through Teach For America, served on our staff, and then worked with Michelle at the New Teacher Project before joining her in D.C. as deputy chancellor. Jason Kamras, who was overseeing the system's teacher-quality initiatives as the director of teacher human-capital strategy, had gained recognition within the Teach For America ranks after eight years of teaching in southeastern D.C., when he was named National Teacher of the Year in 2005. Abigail Smith, a former Teach For America teacher and executive director whom the mayor hired even before he hired Michelle to help reshape the system, was serving as chief transformation officer.

As I asked them about the changes they had been making that might account for the success they were seeing, they emphasized, to use Abby's words, that "a sustainable culture change is the brass ring in this work." In dozens of ways they were working to build a team of individuals who embrace responsibility for clear, positive, ambitious outcomes for kids. As Abby described, "Imagine a deeply rooted, goal-driven approach at the classroom, school, and district levels, where the philosophy *and* the structures are in place to establish goals, measure progress, reflect on success and failure, and change course in response. We're still far from that as a matter of course in DCPS, but we're so much closer than we were three years ago."

To that end, Jason Kamras, who was charged with the responsibility of ensuring a highly effective teacher in every classroom, had been leading efforts to build data systems and learning cycles, just like Joel Klein had been building in New York, that illuminate how teachers are doing in their quest to advance student achievement. He was also managing the growth of professional development systems to ensure that teachers are developing the skills they need to succeed.

To build their teacher performance and support model, Jason and his team drew from a host of models (including Teach For America's Teaching As Leadership framework), conducted dozens of focus groups, and elicited the input of more than five hundred teachers and staff to develop a "Teaching and Learning Framework" that puts forth a vision of teaching excellence and provides descriptions and illustrations of all required skills at various levels of proficiency. They also developed a new evaluation system, called IMPACT, to show teachers where they are against those expectations. IMPACT bases evaluations on a combination of student achievement data, teacher performance ratings on the district's Teaching and Learning Framework, and the degree to which a teacher supports and collaborates with the school and community.

Teachers are reviewed multiple times each year by master educators, whom DCPS hires and trains to conduct teacher observations in their particular areas of expertise and follow up with one-on-one consultations in which they share their ratings and feedback with the observed teachers. Teachers can log on to a Web-based system to access their reviews and receive customized growth plans outlining key strengths, areas for improvement, and next steps for professional development. The IMPACT system is already receiving national attention. Kate Walsh, president of the National Council for Teacher Quality, called it "light years ahead of what's available in most school districts in the United States."[29]

The system's clear articulation of teacher effectiveness is driving the culture that the team wanted to see. Principals have spent considerable time watching and evaluating videos to understand the key teaching strategies that most closely correlate with student achievement. As Abby said, "We now have a set of expectations that are clearly outlined. We all know what we are being held accountable to. This is a major transformation of the conversation for us going forward." Jason agreed, highlighting both the challenges and the opportunities ahead: "We still have lots and lots to do to get there, but now we can work strategically. For the first time ever, we have reliable performance data that will help us figure out how to support our teachers to reach the expectations we've set."

Meanwhile, in New Orleans, a similarly intense emphasis on accountability for student achievement is playing out, though in a different form. Paul Pastorek thinks that setting high expectations that align with his vision of a "world-class education system," and giving strong leaders on each campus the power to innovate around those high expectations as long as they achieve results, is the key to turning things around:

Most people don't believe that we can change the system. We suffer the plague of low expectations in this state and in this city. These expectations are so low that it is hard for us to envision being better. And we blame all kinds of things for why we have what we have. . . . But what we are learning is that there are people who have high expectations, and when you let them in and let them be empowered, we can be successful. . . . If we give people the room to innovate, we attract some really strong people. So at a state-policy level, it is all about setting the bar, measuring it fairly and accurately, and then giving people room to maneuver.

Starting before (but much more aggressively after) Katrina, New Orleans Public Schools embarked on a bold reform movement that has decentralized power from the school board and central office to individual school principals and charter school boards and given parents and families the opportunity to choose from virtually any school in the city. To oversimplify, what "central offices" are left in New Orleans are focused on measuring and monitoring schools' progress, while individual school leaders have the power to make most management decisions in exchange for accountability. The city's system has given the public schools still in the system autonomy and flexibility, including authority to establish curriculum, competitively hire and compensate staff, and contract for basic support services on their campuses.

In New Orleans school leaders and boards are evaluated not on process, just results. They retain their broad autonomy as long as they can demonstrate strong results for students, results measured by a formula that takes into account factors like student achievement, attendance, and dropout rates. Paul Pastorek described the state role to me: "We are taking the bad schools out of business every year, automatically," he said. "If you are going to run a school, we tell you what the goal is, and we give you tools and resources to work with. If your school performs, you don't hear from us. We want to stay out of the way. If it doesn't, someone else is going to run your school."

Over the past decade, Joel Klein had employed, at different times and places, both a centrally driven strategy of school management and an approach that gives schools greater autonomy in exchange for results. Both approaches have demonstrated success in building the culture of accountability that we know is necessary for any large organization of people to be efficient and effective in pursuit of ambitious goals.

A Focus on People

Like the exceptional school leaders we've talked with, successful district leaders like Joel Klein, Paul Pastorek, and Michelle Rhee are united by their conviction that it won't be possible to achieve transformational change without a significant focus on finding, developing, and retaining the right people at every level of the system.

In New Orleans the reform efforts are proving extraordinarily successful in attracting and retaining high-caliber people, and one important factor seems to be the allure of the freedom and autonomy in its highly decentralized system.

When I recently had the opportunity to witness the city's progress firsthand, I was amazed. I remember walking around New Orleans schools years before, sadly realizing just how far behind the students were and how little was being done to change that. But when I visited in the fall of 2010, I walked around school after school where I detected a level of energy and commitment to students that seemed entirely different. I saw dozens of schools led and populated by school leaders and teachers invigorated both by the challenge of building a great education system in the wake of the storm and by the chance to teach and lead without a central office telling them how to do it.

On one of my recent visits to New Orleans, I saw firsthand how autonomy is drawing in strong leaders. On this day I visited what used to be Frances Gregory Middle School, a campus where the impact of Hurricane Katrina on the city's education system was brought into stark relief. Once bustling with 1,000 seventh to tenth graders, today the old, large, partially gutted but still regal school building stands deserted. The building, surrounded by high chain-link fences, had been slated for demolition almost two years ago but still stands, storm damaged and empty.

In Gregory's shadow, right next to those fences, on what before the storm was the school's playground, children are learning and playing in a jumble of spartan FEMA-esque trailers—"modulars," the teachers call them. Though the eleven gray trailers seemed to me indistinguishable from one another, the sign on the chain-link fence showed that they collectively house three separate schools. Three modulars represent the temporary resurrection of Gregory, now as a grades 3–8 school serving several hundred students. This campus is, by design, being phased out of existence as children shift to other schools. The two other campuses, housed in two trailers each, are called Pride College Prep and Akili Academy. Both are new charter schools serving lower-elementary students, schools that will "grow up" with their older students, filling in part of the niche once occupied by the large, mildewing school building beside them. (The remaining modulars are shared by the three schools for a cafeteria, a PE building, a "media center," and a security center.)

As I toured Pride College Prep and Akili Academy with their respective principals, I realized that both of these hard-driving school leaders were drawn to the role because of the unprecedented "room to maneuver" they'd been given. Years before, Akili principal Sean Gallagher had made what felt like a radical move, leaving his original public school classroom to help launch Mastery Charter High School in Philadelphia, now one of the most acclaimed public high schools in that city. When after thirteen years of teaching in

Philadelphia he saw what was happening in New Orleans, he made the decision to uproot himself again, driven by the prospect of working in not just a school but an entire system where school leaders are offered great autonomy in exchange for responsibility for attaining ambitious results. "Post-storm, there was no bureaucracy left, and it really was an open opportunity for people to come down and get schools open quickly, schools that could be designed to close the achievement gap right from the start," he told me.

Meanwhile, just a trailer building away sat Pride College Prep's principal, Michael Richard, who also came to his role because of New Orleans's emphasis on school leadership. A Louisiana native (and philosophy major at Northwestern University), Michael entered education as a kindergarten teacher in Chicago and a year later joined Teach For America in 2003. He taught for three years in a South Side Chicago school before teaching at the American School in Guatemala. In both positions, he led his students to dramatic academic achievement, gaining a reputation as a teacher whose students—whatever their challenges—learn by leaps and bounds.

As Sean and Michael each gave me a tour of his respective school, I saw and met mission-driven teachers drawn into the New Orleans school system by the promise of autonomy to innovate and by the city's explicit appeal to those who want to prove to the country that a truly exceptional urban school district is in fact possible. The teams of people like those at Pride and Akili who are working hard to meet the state's high expectations all over the city represent hundreds and hundreds of new teachers and leaders, many of whom are New Orleans natives and many others who have come from all over the country to be part of what they are sure is a revolutionary and historic transformation.

Without a robust central office in the New Orleans system of schools, a nonprofit called New Schools for New Orleans— founded and run by Teach For America alumna Sarah Newell

Usdin—has stepped in to help manage growth and ensure quality. A few weeks after the storm, I met with Sarah, who years before, in 1992, had been sent to teach fifth grade in Louisiana and never left. She had led the efforts of Teach For America and then the New Teacher Project in the state for years. After the storm, she was personally devastated by the damage to her adopted city and about the work that lay ahead. But she rallied the energy and raised substantial resources to launch New Schools for New Orleans, setting out to attract and support high-performing "human capital" and charter school organizations to enable reform.

The organization works closely with the Recovery School District to attract teachers and principals for New Orleans schools; to incubate, launch, and support open-enrollment public charter schools; and to advocate (and agitate as needed) for accountable and sustainable high-quality public schools. (In fact, both of the two principals I met on my visit to what used to be Frances Gregory Middle School were leaders who had been in New Schools for New Orleans's school-founder "Incubation Program.") New Schools for New Orleans leverages philanthropic money to ensure smart, careful growth of quality leadership and schools, applying the highest expectations and most stringent criteria in deciding which charter applications to recommend to the state. (The organization accepted only 3 percent of applicants to its Incubation Program for new school leaders last year.)

Often with Sarah's help and guidance, some of the country's most successful charter management and school leadership organizations have opened up shop and grown their efforts in New Orleans. The New Teacher Project has brought more than 420 specially selected and trained teachers to high-poverty communities in the city through its "Teach NOLA" initiative, accepting just one in twenty-four applicants through its rigorous screening and training process.[30] New Leaders For New Schools moved into New Orleans and recruited two dozen principals in the three years after the storm.[31] Similarly, at Teach For America—enabled by the growth of our organization and philanthropic support and inspired by the possibilities in New Orleans—we have doubled the size of our corps of teachers in the area to just under five hundred. We are now reaching one in every three New Orleans students and contributing to a critical mass of leaders driven to ensure that New Orleans's children gain the opportunity of an excellent education. By 2012, we will have created a community of a thousand corps members and alumni and we expect there to be at least twenty-five principals in the city who began their careers in education with Teach For America.

When I was last in New Orleans, I was amazed to see how the people-focused changes there had influenced the mindset of our alumni who were placed as teachers in the system many years ago. Andrea Smith Bailey, initially placed in New Orleans as a Teach For America corps member in 1999, assumed she would stay for just two years. Then she fell in love with the city and with teaching, and stayed another year, and another. But only in the past few years has her head, as well as her heart, told her to stay put; Andrea recently decided to buy a house and make New Orleans home. "Teachers know that they are the hottest game in town," she explained. "If you are a good teacher, you know you can find a school where you can really build a career. You can have an income that is workable. You are seeing teacher leadership take on a status that we've always wanted it to have. People not only feel like they are part of something larger than themselves, but they are part of school cultures they want to be part of long-term."

Jay Altman, the CEO of an organization called FirstLine Schools that focuses on turning around failing schools in New Orleans, described the allure of New Orleans to me this way: "It is all about people and leaders. The question then is, what are the conditions that will facilitate a larger pool of people being highly effective as teachers and leaders? We understand the selection effect. You select the most talented people you can. Then there's the development effect—how you develop people. But there is also the *job design* effect. That's the underlying issue that makes success so difficult to achieve for so many educators but where we are extremely fortunate right now in Louisiana. Louisiana is the furthest ahead in terms of giving school leaders space to innovate and focus on the essential work."

It was fascinating to hear this connection between autonomy and attracting and keeping great people in the system. With this approach, New Orleans is not just attracting and retaining more Teach For America alumni but also surfacing the talent already present in the school system. One of our alumni, Jim Furman, now an assistant professor in the education school at the University of New Orleans, told me, "I do think there are school leaders who were among the best in the city who are now leading schools and are still among the best in the city. There are also school leaders who were good and have become great—in some cases because autonomy has allowed them the opportunity and in some cases because the expectations have been raised. And there are school leaders who are demonstrating success and were not school leaders before the storm." He explained several reasons for the shift toward excellence, first among them being a redefinition of success or what is expected in terms of demonstrable performance:

> As a classroom teacher I was often judged by the noise level of my classroom and whether or not students were on task when an administrator walked by. I believe the same was true for school leaders. Performance was judged on the number of discipline problems, and the reputation of schools was based largely on the perception that the principal was able to maintain control. At the school level and the

classroom level, this was all about the *perception* of learning or having the environment in place where learning could theoretically occur. Now, the focus is on *actual* learning. It seems that principals know that success under the old definition isn't enough to cut it anymore, and they now have more models of what a great school can look like. The best have known that all along, but are now in a situation where they have the autonomy and power to address learning and instruction, rather than issues of discipline and management. The job has shifted from building manager to instructional leader. There are many principals in the city who had that skill set and now have much more power to actually impact instruction because of the autonomy they are allowed.

The other developments Jim identified were an improved principal appointment system (today's principals are chosen based on merit, without the favoritism and rigidity exhibited in the previous era) and the authority of principals to recruit and develop their own teachers and to manage their own budgets.

In Washington, D.C., we have seen an intense focus on people as well. Michelle told me a story about one of her teachers saying to her, "You know, I don't mind at all being evaluated and being held to high standards of effectiveness, as long as that comes with high standards of support and professional development." "That's exactly right," she said to me. "We want to create a system that expects a lot at the same time that it provides a lot. Traditionally, the supports teachers have received have been fragmented, inconsistent, and unclear. We aspire to change that."

As the mayor's term ended, both the evaluation system and the support and development system were in their nascent stages. It remains to be seen whether and how Michelle's vision will be realized, but her hard-charging focus on the effectiveness of D.C. teachers and administrators created shock waves well beyond the nation's capital. A few weeks into her tenure she insisted on the right to hire and fire her central staff and made significant changes within the central office. In her first year, Michelle replaced a quarter of the system's 150 principals.[32]

Michelle also proposed a new teachers' contract that she felt would increase the caliber of the teaching force. This contract, now ratified by the teachers' union, provides district teachers a 21.6 percent salary increase through 2012, raising the average salary of D.C. educators from $67,000 to about $81,000, which is near the top of the pay scale for teachers in the D.C. metropolitan region. It offers teachers higher compensation in exchange for greater accountability for their students' academic growth: The teachers who are involved in the pay-for-performance system will make as much as $130,000 a year if they can show better than expected growth in student test scores and hit other targets. The contract also allows principals to use performance, instead of seniority, as the chief determinant when reducing staff, and it stipulates that displaced teachers are no longer guaranteed spots in the system. Under a "mutual consent" clause, teachers and principals must both agree to a transfer, instead of teachers being slotted into open positions by the central office.

While the full implications of this contract were still unknown as I was finishing this book, it seems to be making D.C. a competitive and attractive player in the fight for education talent. At the same time, the contract is enabling the system to remove teachers who aren't serving students well. A few months after this contract was signed, DCPS dismissed about 4 percent of teachers (165 teachers) based on poor performance.

Though the approaches in D.C., New Orleans, and New York have all been different, these improving systems are all placing their bets in the same place: on attracting and developing committed, capable people at every level of the system. Given what we've learned about successful classrooms and schools, this bodes well for the future of these school systems.

○ ○ ○

THE EFFORTS AND OUTCOMES in New York City, New Orleans, and Washington, D.C., shed light on the necessary ingredients for systemwide reform. Although it is too early to know whether one particular governance structure is a prerequisite for reform, it is clear that the path to better outcomes starts with a vision for transformational change through education and a commitment to the long, hard work involved in building highly effective organizations in pursuit of meaningful change.

LESSON 3:
LEADERSHIP, LEADERSHIP, LEADERSHIP: SUCCESS WILL TAKE TRANSFORMATIONAL LEADERSHIP AT EVERY LEVEL

These improving school systems show us not only that progress is possible but what success requires. The distinguishing and driving factor in all the places where whole systems are turning around is transformational leadership—leaders who view their responsibility and education itself as putting children in low-income communities on a different track in life and who commit to doing whatever it takes to accomplish this end.

In New Orleans, Paul Pastorek and Paul Vallas are providing precisely this type of transformational leadership, and they have created a system that attracts and retains similar leaders in classrooms and on school campuses throughout New Orleans. D.C. mayor Adrian Fenty, who himself insisted that education could and should be a primary lever against the cycle of poverty in his city, chose Michelle Rhee because she too was a transformational leader.

Michelle, in turn, surrounded herself with other transformational leaders and put systems in place to attract and retain such leadership on her campuses and in her classrooms. And in New York City, where these reforms have been under way most aggressively over the longest period of time, we also see the presence of transformational leadership at every level.

I recently had an eye-opening experience in what has to be one of the toughest educational contexts in the nation that verified for me that transformational leadership is the linchpin of the massively difficult and complex work of turning around entire systems. I went to meet with Cami Anderson, one of our alumni who is managing District 79, a still centrally controlled district within New York City's larger system, that is charged with supporting students on the verge of dropping out of the system. If success is possible in her district, we know it is possible everywhere. The young adults the district serves are among those most in need of extra support. Of the 90,000 students who come through the district each year, 60,000 are over the age of twenty-one, and many of them face extraordinary challenges, from being a pregnant teen to incarceration to drug addiction to family trauma.

Four years into his tenure as chancellor, Joel Klein appointed Cami to run District 79. He saw her entrepreneurial leadership and take-no-excuses approach as critical to the system's turnaround. Cami insists that education must mean more than making resources available to students and mere test scores; she insists that the role of education is to put students on a different path in life than they are on when they first show up.

I accompanied Cami on one of her frequent school visits. On this day she was going to Passages Academy, a school embedded in a "secure facility" run by the Department of Juvenile Justice and serving students awaiting trials, sentencing, and other court appearances. Because their placement is driven by the adjudication process, students enter and exit the system frequently. Passages Academy serves about 2,000 mostly eighth and ninth graders over the course of a year and approximately 400 on any given day. The average time spent at Passages is about thirty school days, though many students are there for just a few days and others are there for an entire year. Of the students served by Passages, 30 percent end up being sent upstate to prison, and 70 percent return to their communities and to their home schools.

As we made our way through the metal detectors and cell-like locked chambers at the entrance of the school, Cami described what she encountered upon taking over District 79. When she began, no one seemed to know how many *schools* there were in the district, let alone how many students were being served. She could not find anyone who knew how many employees were on the payroll. Cami explained that the most critical questions, like what students' academic needs were and to what degree they were being met, were not even being asked, much less answered.

When she arrived, Cami found a pervasive culture of resignation—a perspective rationalized by the massive challenges facing the district's students. "People would tell me that having something like 12 percent of kids graduate—even though we had no way of actually knowing whether that number was right—was wonderful because these kids likely wouldn't be in school at all," Cami told me. "Sure, any percent is better than no percent, but the fact is that we were—and still are—failing the majority of our kids. It is dangerous when adults tell themselves, 'We should be commended no matter what because we're serving the kids that no one else wants.'" I know Cami well enough to imagine her reaction to hearing such a sentiment. She does not suffer low expectations lightly. I first saw her exemplify high standards and leadership when she served as executive director of our New York region, now almost ten years ago.

Cami's take-charge toughness and determination to insist that children with the greatest needs get the most support were developed while growing up in a family of fourteen. Nine of her siblings were adopted, and many of them joined her family facing some of the same life challenges her schools are addressing in District 79. Two of Cami's siblings, both of whom are doing well now, actually received their diplomas in involuntary settings like Passages Academy.

Cami entered the field of education as a Teach For America corps member in Los Angeles in 1993. She taught thirty-eight sixth graders without the support of a supplementary school aide. Attending the lowest-performing school in the district, many of Cami's students had been kicked out of their previous schools or classrooms for "extreme behavior." As one of those early Teach For America teachers who brought incredible leadership to their classrooms, Cami made extraordinary gains with her students. In fact, on various student assessments, her students outpaced the learning of any other class in the district. Cami's success earned her district's sole nomination for a national Sallie Mae Teacher of the Year award. Her personal experiences have strengthened Cami's conviction that children facing inordinate challenges can in fact make dramatic academic progress and deepened her understanding of what success requires.

As I listened to Cami explain, without a hint of doubt, that District 79 could and would become a place where students leave more ready to succeed in school and life than they were when they arrived, I heard echoes of the other successful system leaders we've met. Education is, she believes, about changing lives:

> Our students—those who have met tremendous obstacles—
> need a transformational and recuperative experience that not
> only allows them to obtain the critical credentials necessary
> to access life options but that gives them the competence,
> confidence, and sense of urgency to succeed. A teen parent
> or a young person with a criminal record and no high school
> diploma and without the requisite critical thinking/speaking/

writing skills that diploma should represent has very limited
life options. A teen parent or a young person with a criminal
record with exceptional literacy, numeracy, and higher-order
thinking skills (combined with their ability to persist in the
face of obstacles) and a high school diploma has countless options. I believe education is critical for opening doors for all of
our kids—it is life critical for the kids in District 79.

As a series of massive metal doors buzzed and clanked to allow
us to enter Passages Academy, Cami summed up her hard-earned
philosophy as superintendent of District 79: "When kids who are
facing extreme challenges get more of what they need in terms of
academic and social and emotional support—and less of what they
don't need in terms of low expectations—they absolutely can make
significant academic gains. We have to show them that we believe
in them by expecting excellence. For young people who have experienced consistent failure, that's everything: knowing an adult believes in them even when they have given up on themselves."

Cami described for me the reasons young people end up in a place
like District 79: Some encounter adults who convince them they cannot achieve, some make bad decisions that get them in serious trouble,
some experience major tragedy in their families, and some are
wrestling with all of these challenges. "Yet, despite seemingly insurmountable odds, many of our young people show extraordinary determination and a desire to turn things around," Cami says. "At
fourteen, fifteen years old, or twenty-two, they are often openly reflecting on who they are, what others think of them, and where they
want to be. Many, with a little help, are ready to start anew. We have
to grab that window of opportunity and put them on different paths."

Cami, just like other district leaders who are turning around
large ships, begins with a vision for changing student trajectories.
She wants students in District 79 to have a transformational educa-

tional experience that will make them better students and citizens who have the broadest range of life options available to them—an audacious goal, she acknowledges, that will take years to realize.

And, just like Michelle, Paul, and Joel, Cami's first order of business when she came to District 79 was to build a team of people who shared her vision of the district and her belief in its students. Cami closed and reconstituted a number of schools, rehiring only about half of the teachers previously employed in the district. She simultaneously shrank and changed the composition of the central office, pushing resources and people to the students in the schools. "We have to surround our students with teachers, and surround teachers with managers, who expect our students to succeed—and have the vision and skill to help them do it," she said.

On the day I visited Cami's school, however, her primary focus was on an equally important priority: helping this influx of leaders understand exactly what they are accountable for. Just as Michelle Rhee did, Cami made a point of sitting down with all of the principals in her first months on the job to crisply define their respective responsibilities and goals. Like Michelle, Cami expects her principals to arrange target-setting conversations with the teachers they manage and, on any given day, be familiar with and actively support their teachers' progress toward their goals. "We *have* to be clear about what we are aiming for," she said. With an overworked team of two data specialists, Cami has created a data "dashboard" for each site and each program designed to track key aspects of students' successes and failures, including student achievement results and attendance data. "Whether students are learning, and how much, should be driving all of our decisions," Cami said. "The last thing our students want to hear is 'Someday you'll get your GED.' They want to hear 'Look, today you are here. If you work hard, tomorrow, you'll be *here*. Then we can get you to this step, this is the path to a GED, and here is how that can help you get into college.' In many ways we are all really simple: We want to know what success looks like, we want to have ways of measuring our success, and we want to feel like it's clear how to progress."

Cami has built a culture of accountability not only for teachers but for students. She has instituted a "success-o-meter" process in which students track their progress against key goals. Cami told me about one recent interaction with an incarcerated student, who told her, "I thought this whole thing was so cheesy, but then I saw my meter go way below 50 percent in every goal. I had to basically say to myself, 'Am I going to man up and push that bar higher, or am I going to come back to the table next Friday and see my dial drop below 50 percent?'"

Like the other leaders I have profiled in this chapter, Cami is far from satisfied with where her system is on its most important measures, but she is willing to smile about some early indicators of success. Last year, nearly 7,000 students in District 79 were enrolled in a GED program. While the district is now serving many more students who lag behind their peers across the city, the percentage of students who sit for and pass the GED has tripled since she arrived. Of those students who sat for the GED exam last school year, 80 percent passed, compared with 60 percent in 2006 and the 47 percent pass rate statewide. Cami has also developed engaging short-term courses that lead to viable career options for her students throughout the district—such as a licensed practical nurse training program that has a 90 percent passing rate and guarantees graduates a position in a New York City hospital and a program offering certificates in "green construction" developed in partnership with Solar One, so students can get ahead in emerging job markets.

The story of District 79 is powerful for several reasons. It shows that progress is possible in even the most challenging contexts. It shows that the same fundamental building blocks of effective organizations anywhere are also key to turning around dysfunctional school systems. Above all, District 79 shows us the power of transformational leadership. Cami—as part of a chain of command including the mayor, the chancellor, her principals, and her teachers—is acting on her conviction that poverty, with all of its inherent challenges, does not have to win. These transformational leaders know that with a lot of hard work and attention to the fundamentals of effective organization building, education can trump poverty.

CONCLUSION

The leaders who are changing whole school systems show great discipline in communicating a clear, unifying, inspiring, and ambitious vision of a system that enables children to fulfill their potential; implementing systems of management, support, and accountability that ensure alignment and effectiveness for every member of the team; and making the recruitment and development of great people a primary, high-investment part of the system. At the same time, their choices indicate that many of the ideas and interventions that we spend most of our time debating are not actually the keys to success.

I remember meeting a longtime leader in education who was expressing concerns about how Michelle Rhee was doing a few months into her tenure. "Where is her instructional plan?" he asked. Michelle had not rolled out a new instructional plan because she did not believe that the instructional plan was what was holding D.C. schools back. Whereas the person asking this question viewed curricular reform as a standard part of any new superintendent's agenda, from Michelle's perspective a new curriculum would be close to meaningless if it was implemented without completely changing the system's culture—the way that people in it are managed, inspired, and supported to ensure student motivation and learning.

While transformational leaders like Joel Klein, Cami Anderson, Michelle Rhee, and Paul Pastorek are showing us what will be required over time to build whole systems of transformational schools, their choices of what to prioritize also help us understand the limitations of other reform efforts. To this point, the next chapter will explore why we haven't seen even more progress in the aggregate educational data despite all the focus on improving education over the last two decades.

4

SILVER BULLETS AND SILVER SCAPEGOATS

IN 2006 THE BEAUTIFULLY DESIGNED $62 million–dollar boldly named "School of the Future" opened in Philadelphia. The brainchild of a team of experts at a major technology company, this school was heralded as a revolution in education. The plans were exciting: laptops for every student, innovative scheduling, "twenty-first-century" course design, and online courses and resources.

The energy around the school was positive and infectious. Before it was even built, some were talking about its potential for replication across the country. I remember thinking, and even saying to an executive at the company at the time, I hope the folks who are designing this have spent some time in the (at that time few) high-performing new schools in low-income communities to understand what really accounts for their success.

I don't believe they had. At least so far, the school's results have been deeply disappointing. On the 2009 Pennsylvania assessments, only 8 percent of the school's eleventh graders were deemed proficient in math (compared to 32 percent of students citywide and 56 percent of students statewide). Only 23 percent met proficiency standards in reading (compared to 38 percent of students citywide and 65 percent statewide). Perhaps most shocking, here at a school based on technological innovation, only 2 percent of its students met proficiency standards in science (compared to 7 percent citywide and 40 percent statewide). The one bright spot for the school was its writing results, the only area where the school outperformed the rest of the city. In this area, 66 percent of students demonstrated at least proficiency, whereas across Philadelphia 64 percent of students met that mark.[1]

How is it that despite its gorgeous design, tens of millions of dollars of investment, and state-of-the-art technology, the School of the Future is being dramatically outperformed by the schools it was meant to replace? I recently visited the school and saw how, in the absence of a transformative mission and without the leadership, team, culture, effective management, and extra student supports to act on that mission, the technology that was meant to revolutionize the school was in fact having a *negative* impact. Not only had the technology diverted the school's designers from the core work that actually accounts for strong schools, but it was actually distracting the students. In the classroom I visited, as the teacher attempted to talk loudly through the day's lesson, I watched from the back of the room as literally every kid in the class either surfed the Internet, played computer games, sent instant messages to friends, or, in the cases of a couple of students, attempted to fix broken computers. The scene was appalling. It would have seemed almost comical if the stakes for these children hadn't been so high.

It is useful, I think, to reflect on this example as we consider dozens of other interventions. Charters, small schools, small classes, and longer school days—to name a few—have all been heralded as ways to save our education system. Each could play an important role, if implemented by leaders driving toward a vision for transformational change who understand what it takes to build and manage high-performing organizations. Outside of that context, each runs the risk of serving as an unfortunate distraction of energy.

I believe part of the reason that the achievement gap has not narrowed in an aggregate sense over the past two decades, despite all the energy and resources invested in education reform, is that our policy makers and influencers have been so obsessed with finding a quick fix that we have gone lurching from one silver-bullet solution to another rather than embracing the big idea of transformative education and engaging in the very hard work of implementing it. Equally distracting, we have also spent inordinate amounts of energy blaming one group or another—"silver scapegoats," we could call them—when there are clearly larger systemic issues at play. The fact is that our system was not initially designed with an understanding of what it would take to change the path predicted by students' socioeconomic background. Given the resulting systemic issues, blaming any one set of people in the system really does not make sense. Even worse, it will only lead those groups, whose deep engagement and leadership we so desperately need, to feel frustrated and unvalued.

THE COSTLY FIXATION ON SILVER BULLETS

The urgency of the achievement gap makes us yearn for a quick fix that will close it. Yet everything we are learning from the most successful classrooms, schools, charter management organizations, and districts proves that there are no shortcuts.

It's Not All About More Funding

Several years ago, I had the opportunity to take a presidential candidate on a tour of KIPP Gaston Prep, a school in rural North Carolina that was showing record-breaking results with a population of students living at or near the poverty line. The school is a picture of simplicity. Like so many of the highest-performing charter schools in the country, only minimal and necessary attention was put into the school building itself, and the school is working with fewer dollars per pupil than traditional schools.

Launched in 2001 as the third school in the KIPP network, KIPP Gaston Prep has a student body that is 86 percent African American, with more than 65 percent of its students qualifying for free or reduced lunch. Although it was opened as a middle school, it quickly evolved into an institution serving fifth through twelfth grades. The results are impressive: In the first two high school graduating classes, the classes of 2009 and 2010, 100 percent of seniors were accepted to college.[2]

I watched as the presidential candidate questioned Caleb Dolan and Tammi Sutton, the Teach For America alumni who had pioneered the school's development. He just didn't believe they could achieve the results they did with the same level of funding as the school down the road. Caleb persisted patiently, explaining that actually they were spending only 85 percent as much as the other school since their allocation of public dollars was less.

Throughout the morning, the candidate's skepticism remained strong. During lunch, however, I wondered if it might be dissipating. Caleb and Tammi had invited some of the students' parents to come to the school at lunchtime for an informal discussion. Listening to the parents, it became clear that the school was actually breaking the cycle of poverty. The parents were describing the change in their children—the fact that their children were now waking *them* up to make sure they got to school on time. One parent explained that thanks to this school, he knew he would retire in comfort.

As we sat down in the plane to go back home, the candidate said, "This visit really made an impact on me." I was surprised, and he continued: "It had never actually occurred to me that this might not be a resources issue—that actually, it's about believing in the kids."

Politicians, parents, and school leaders often point to funding as the critical issue. In fact, when we visited the middle school a couple of miles away from KIPP Gaston Prep, the entire focus of the faculty's discussion with the candidate was their concern about insufficient financial resources.

Constraining resources certainly play a role in limiting what a school can do, and in some states it is a much greater barrier than in others. In California, for example, the state spends not much more than half what is spent in some other states on a per-pupil basis, and leaders of all types of schools agree that more money is necessary to be successful. Many of the high-performing charter schools, for example, have found it unrealistic to live within the dollars allocated by the state, so they expend considerable energy seeking other sources of funding.

But I am seeing in schools and districts across the country that it is usually a mistake to assume that more money is "the answer." Even as it is true that we need to invest more in our schools, some schools are getting dramatically different results with the same amounts of money—and in many cases some of the most effective schools are spending less than some of the least-effective schools.

Over the thirty-five-year span from 1970 to 2005, inflation-adjusted per-pupil spending doubled.[3] Yet we have seen spotty NAEP score improvements over that time and no meaningful growth in SAT scores.[4] According to a McKinsey and Company study on the achievement gap, the United States comes in *dead last* in school-spending cost-effectiveness (as measured in math scores) among OECD (Organization for Economic Co-operation and Development) countries.[5]

Given how much we'll need to invest to develop world-class human capital systems and technology systems and to provide students with the supports they need to get transformational results, I think it may well prove important to increase the resources invested in education if we are going to get exceptional results at scale. As we gain the capability to track not "dollars per pupil" but "dollars per successful pupil," our understanding of the true cost of doing what works will become more apparent. Moreover, we will need to be much smarter about allocating the funding we have. Right now, we have a funding system that does not generally invest more dollars—let alone equal dollars—in meeting the extra needs of its most disadvantaged kids.

I remember Tammi Sutton herself, at KIPP Gaston, describing the need for investing more in education in urban and rural areas back when I was visiting her classroom to understand how she was attaining transformational results as a teacher. At the end of a long day, she put it succinctly when she said, "I'm not trying to give my kids the same education that kids in the privileged community next door have access to. I'm trying to give them more. My kids face extra challenges, and equal inputs won't generate equal outcomes." But at the same time, a lack of resources need not be an excuse for the status quo, and we need to be clear that more resources don't automatically generate better outcomes.

The Limitations of Structural Changes Like Charters, Vouchers, and School Size

Over the years, I have found myself in countless discussions with those who are deeply committed to education reform and are convinced that restructuring the school system is the answer. They make a compelling argument. As we've seen in the examples of New Orleans and New York City, structural change can be a powerful enabler of reform. Changes that empower leaders with flexibility over inputs in exchange for accountability for outcomes, or that give parents choice over where to take their educational dollars, can be crucial levers. In D.C., the market pressure created by a growing charter school movement—which had attracted almost a third of the D.C. system's students[6]—contributed to the climate that made it possible for the mayor and chancellor to pursue such a bold agenda.

What we've seen in the communities where we work, however, is that these changes will get us only so far. If tomorrow we lifted all the policy barriers to progress but we had failed to develop the leadership and capacity to run transformational schools, we would not actually change our educational outcomes in a way that is meaningful for children.

Take the experience of the charter school movement. As we've seen, the charter model of school governance gives schools freedom from district rules and management in exchange for accepting accountability for certain results agreed upon in the "charter." As described in Chapter 2, charter laws have played a critical role in providing the opportunity for committed leaders to create schools that serve students well. But without equal commitment to building the leadership and capacity to take advantage of those laws, the overall charter movement has not generated the desired results. There are more than 5,000 charter schools operating in the United States, responsible for the education of more than 1.5 million children.[7] When we look across the field of charter schools, we see vast variation in effectiveness—from exceptionally successful to dismally failing. According to one study out of Stanford, more than one-third of charter schools nationally are providing an education that is "significantly worse" than comparable local schools.[8] On average, charter schools aren't yet doing better than traditional schools according to the preponderance of the research.

Those who view charter schools as a silver bullet that will save urban education are drawing the wrong conclusion from successful charter schools like those found in the KIPP, Achievement First, Mastery, and Uncommon Schools networks. It's not freedom from district rules, per se, that leads to success—though that freedom is a critical enabler. It is, rather, the quality of the school leadership teams and what they do with their latitude. Too often, those who have championed charter laws haven't spent enough energy on building the supports and making the investments necessary to propagate great options for kids.

Leslie Jacobs—the longtime advocate of educational change in New Orleans—has seen the power of charter schools to transform education. But she cautions against assuming that it is the "charter" that drives the success. "One hundred percent of a school's success is the quality of the leader and the teachers," she told me. "But the charters are a leverage point. If you are good, the autonomy of charters allows you to be great in ways that would be hard to achieve in a traditional system. On the other hand, if you are average or below, you are likely to be a little worse in a charter school because you have so many more responsibilities."

With that perspective, Leslie laments the pressure—which she successfully helped resist—to "flip" failing traditional public schools in New Orleans into charters without having the talent-development pipelines in place to staff those schools with leaders who will get the job done. Jacobs is no fan of failing schools, but she recognizes that strong leaders and hard work, not simply the independence granted by a charter, make great schools. "Ensuring quality—and that's what we have to have—takes time," she told me. "The first year after Katrina, we only approved six of forty-four applications for charters because those were the ones that had the leadership and people and plans to be successful. The commitment to quality has to have a long-term view. We took the time to develop high-quality new charter operators and the necessary school leadership."

The voucher, or "school choice," movement—a policy initiative to give parents the financial resources to choose public or private schools for their children—proves a similar point. I find it hard to argue with any policy that gives low-income parents the option to choose a new school when their assigned school is clearly failing its students. In New Orleans and in parts of New York City where parents can choose their public schools, we've seen firsthand that parental choice increases schools' accountability for results and engages and empowers parents in important ways. That said, vouchers produce transformational change for children and families only if there are really good schools where the vouchers can be used, and there's simply no way around the hard work of creating those schools.

Despite high hopes that the market pressure created in a voucher system would improve outcomes for children by creating competition among schools, the empirical evidence around voucher success is somewhat mixed and, where positive, suggests only incremental impact. An April 2010 study of Milwaukee's program, where approximately 20,000 students are using taxpayer dollars to attend one of about 130 private schools, found that students in the voucher program performed no better than students in the regular school system.[9] A study of the Washington, D.C., voucher program, conducted by the U.S. Department of Education, likewise found no conclusive evidence that vouchers affect student achievement, though it did determine that the voucher program significantly increased the odds that a student would graduate from high school.[10] And a 2003 study by the conservative think tank the Manhattan Institute for Policy Research reported an additional benefit—namely, schools facing a heightened level of competition from vouchers made significantly better improvements than those that did not face such competition.[11] So vouchers, championed by some as the key to saving our education system, are turning out to have some meaningful impact but not anything like the transformation we need.

Another effort to change educational outcomes through addressing the structure of the system took place in the early 2000s when the Bill and Melinda Gates Foundation spent somewhere in the neighborhood of $2 billion on its "small schools" initiative. The theory was that smaller, more autonomous schools would better serve students than the large high schools where students can easily get lost. With the foundation's funding fueling this effort, 2,600 "small schools" were created, either as brand-new enterprises or often by reconstituting existing large high schools into smaller programs.[12]

Today, many of the large urban high schools I visit that used to have one name now have three or four names, each with a different thematic focus. Maurice Thomas, the exceptional teacher in Atlanta introduced in the first chapter, worked at the "School for Technology, Engineering, Math, and Science at Therrell," for example—a small school on the Therrell campus that shares a cafeteria and gym with three other "small schools."

There is much about the idea of smaller schools that is appealing. Given that schools' quality is so very much influenced by their leadership, and given that we simply do not have strong-enough leaders to manage all the complexities of massive schools, it could in fact be easier at this moment in history to build a lot of great small schools. On the flip side, it is challenging to find that many more great leaders. But like any other structural intervention, small schools transform students' education experience only when the reconfigurations are coupled with an intense, and much more difficult, focus on building transformational schools in the way that we saw at Port Houston Elementary, WHEELS in New York, KIPP Heartwood in San Jose, and North Star in Newark.

Indeed, the results of the small schools movement have been disappointing, according to a Gates-funded study of its own programs.[13] "Simply breaking up existing schools into smaller units often did not generate the gains we were hoping for," said Bill Gates as he reflected on the small schools movement. He continued:

> It's clear that you can't dramatically increase college readiness by changing only the size and structure of a school. The schools that made dramatic gains in achievement did the changes in design and also emphasized changes inside the classroom. . . . In general, the places that demonstrated the strongest results tended to do many proven reforms well, all at once: they would create smaller schools, a longer day, better relationships—but they would also establish college-ready standards aligned with a rigorous curriculum, with the instructional tools to support it, effective teachers to teach it, and data systems to track the progress.[14]

The Limitations of Changing Inputs Like Class Size, Curriculum, Technology, and . . . Field Trips

While some have embraced structural reforms as "the answer," others have focused their energy on one classroom intervention or another, again to disappointing effect. For years, for example, class-size reduction has been touted as a panacea for our ailing education system. Over the past decade, as much as 57 percent annually of the billions of Title II education funding dollars from the federal government went to "class size reduction."[15]

Of course, small classes can be a real benefit to student learning when the classes have strong teachers. An oft-cited Tennessee study found strong positive benefits of class-size reduction (comparing classes of thirteen to seventeen students per teacher versus those with twenty-two to twenty-five students per teacher).[16] When class-size reduction becomes state or federal policy in the absence of more fundamental changes that expand the pipeline of effective teachers, however, there are unintended consequences.

In 1996 California announced a plan to dramatically reduce class size. Yet without an effective corresponding effort to recruit or develop more excellent teachers, this policy did not go well for the children of California. According to a consortium hired by the state to study the effects of the policy, there was no clear link between class-size reductions and academic gains.[17] The costs to the system increased significantly with no payoff in terms of student learning.

Like class size, many curricular reforms—project-based curricula, scripted curricula, "whole language" versus "phonics" literacy curricula—have been and are touted as the key to success. And, in some cases, the right curriculum has been shown to have a positive impact (though still only a fraction of the transformative impact necessary to close the achievement gap).[18] Yet no curriculum is good enough to overcome bad teaching. And in some cases, heavily scripted curricula suppress great teaching in an effort to raise the floor of poor teaching.

We should continue investigating and investing in building strong resources and curricula for teachers, but successful classrooms and schools reveal that particular curricula are not the distinguishing factor in success. Unless a curriculum is surrounded by the fundamental elements of a purposeful, high-functioning organization, it will not by itself transform student learning.

The same can be said of technology-enhanced learning. Many have looked to technology as the answer to our failing schools. In fact, we desperately need to revolutionize the way schools work, and as I will discuss in the next chapter, technology—when placed in the context of all the other fixes that are required—has the potential to provide useful leverage to those who are working to build high-performing systems. But again, the technological innovations can be valuable only if used *in the service of* transformational class-rooms and schools—not as a replacement for them.

A February 2009 study by the National Center for Education Evaluation showed that educational software did not impact student learning. Further analysis of the study's findings shows that the results may reflect a lack of school-level and classroom-level execution of the software programs rather than their effectiveness when used regularly, providing further evidence that while technology can be part of the solution, it is not a panacea.

I have been in some exceptional learning environments that are not using any technology at all and in some exceptionally poor learning environments that are using a lot of technology: "smart boards" where teachers' notes are automatically transferred to soft copy; PowerPoint presentations, videos, and graphics on screens; or laptops for children's use. Like so many other interventions in education, various technological tools can make good teachers better, but can also make less effective teachers worse, as we saw in the classroom I observed at the School of the Future. Apple Computer's Steve Jobs put it well: "It is so much more hopeful to think that technology can solve the problems that are more human and more organizational and more political in nature, and it ain't so. We need to attack these things at the root, which is people and how much freedom we give people, the competition that will attract the best people," he said. "I feel very strongly about this. I wish it was as simple as giving it over to the computer."[19]

An even more popular fixation of late is the idea of requiring students to spend more time in schools. As we've seen from the most successful classrooms and schools, putting children in low-income areas on a level playing field requires more time. As it is, most highly effective teachers and schools find ways to extend the learning day. We've also seen that the "summer slide" is a real problem, as students lose the progress they have made. And there are reasons to provide children in urban and rural areas with safe and nurturing places for longer than the day and school year allow.

Yet it is still worrisome to see policy makers look at high-performing schools with longer days and conclude that more time is "the" answer, or even one powerful answer absent any other changes. Perhaps this seems obvious, yet I find it absolutely remarkable how often our policy makers and influencers try to make answers simpler than they really are.

A few years ago, I met with the new superintendent of one of the nation's largest school systems in his first week. He explained to me his agenda for change, which had three planks. One of the three was to provide more field trips across this massive school system. He told me he had looked at the KIPP model and concluded that what made it successful was the fact that KIPP exposes its students to new opportunities that many other low-income students cannot access. In fact, KIPP does have a system of rewards whereby students take trips at the end of each grade to visit colleges and places of national importance. This is a wonderful aspect of KIPP, yet it was sad to hear this superintendent, who was responsible for the education of hundreds of thousands of children, draw the conclusion that this was one of three things that would be most critical in a school system that wasn't even graduating—let alone ensuring the success of—half of its children.

The Maurice Thomases and Chris Barbics and Michelle Rhees of the world might not agree on everything. They might come from different points on the political spectrum. But as educators in high-need communities who have attained results that are transformational for their students, they share a deep knowledge that there is no "one thing" that accounts for success. There are no shortcuts. This is about the long, hard work entailed in effecting significant change and important results in any field.

The Newest Silver Bullet: Providing
Every Child with an Effective Teacher

Recent studies are showing that teachers—highly effective teachers—are a massive lever for influencing the achievement gap. One study found that when a group of second grade students received a top-quartile teacher for three straight years, they ended up performing at the 83rd percentile nationally. This kind of progress would put those students squarely in reach of college and give them a shot at college scholarships. When a similar group of second graders, however, was given a bottom-quartile teacher for three straight years, they ended up at the 29th percentile nationally, squarely in the population of students likely to drop out of school.[20] In another study, low-income students in classrooms with the top 5 percent of teachers had accomplished a year and a half's worth of learning in a single school year, while students taught by the bottom 5 percent advanced only a half year in the same period.[21] In the world of classroom interventions, we just do not see impacts of this magnitude. Highly effective teachers can, as we have seen, be transformative.

The conclusion of many philanthropists and policy makers has been, naturally enough, that we should focus on ensuring that every student has a highly effective teacher. Bill Gates and his foundation's leadership, for example, have come away from his small schools initiative with an intense focus on effective teaching:

Great teaching is the centerpiece of a strong education; everything else revolves around it. This is the main finding of our foundation's work in education over the past ten years. I have to admit—that is not where we started. Our work in schools began with a focus on making high schools smaller, in the hope of improving relationships to drive down dropout rates and increase student achievement. Many of the schools we worked with made strong gains, but others were disappointing. The schools that made the biggest gains in achievement did more than make structural changes; they also improved teaching.[22]

Gates and others rightly appreciate that strong teaching is a non-negotiable foundation for a great education system. However, many who are focused on improving teaching see the challenge we face as engineering the production of 3.7 million transformative teachers. We do need to ensure that every child has a highly effective teacher, but if we take this on absent other changes, we run the risk that efforts to improve teaching will also prove disappointing. As I've tried to bring to life in previous chapters, it is hard to envision the path to 3.7 million teachers performing at high levels without overhauling the larger context in which they are working. It is a very rare person who can be a transformational teacher outside of a transformational school.

Teach For America is in the luxurious position of being able to field a relatively small corps of rare leaders, and thanks to immense time and energy spent developing a data-driven selection system and continuously improving the training and professional development we provide our recruits, independent studies reveal that our teachers have a positive impact, sometimes even compared to veteran teachers. Yet despite all these investments, our teachers are still not, on average, changing the trajectory of their students in a truly meaningful way. With a lot of hard work, we are getting better, but we are not where we need to be: The bell curve of effectiveness within our corps is still too wide. While I deeply believe in the importance of expanding Teach For America, not only because our teachers are having a positive impact during their two-year commitments but also because of the long-term value of influencing the mindsets and career paths of our corps members, our experience should provide a sobering perspective on the idea that we can "fix" our education system through a single-minded focus on teachers.

And it would be misguided to assume that there's an as-of-yet undiscovered route for teacher preparation or retaining excellent teachers that will prove to be the silver bullet. There is no evidence, for example, that longer preservice training, teacher residencies that place new teachers as apprentices for a year before they assume full-time teaching positions, or incentives for teachers to stay in the classroom longer produce significant impacts.

It is true that we must think of our challenge as ensuring that students who are far behind have multiple years of exposure to highly effective teachers. But finding, selecting, developing, supporting, and retaining a teaching force as effective as our top quartile of teachers today will require serious systemic changes. As we have seen, the growing number of schools in this country that are accomplishing this feat are doing so by embracing a transformational mission and building the culture, accountability system, management structure, and talent pipeline necessary to fulfill it.

Yes, at the end of the day, children's lives will be transformed by the classroom leaders who facilitate their academic achievements. We are right to focus on teachers, but the most promising way to increase the sheer numbers of effective teachers is to change the whole system—to foster the school-level aspirations, leadership, cultures, and people-development and -management systems that make it easier for teachers to succeed. Unfortunately, there is no shortcut.

○ ○ ○

THE ACHIEVEMENT GAP IN AMERICA is massive. If we think in terms of mapping student performance on a one hundred–point scale, the black-white achievement gap appears to be about thirty-five points.

Meanwhile, virtually all of the strategies mentioned in this chapter, even if we accept only the most optimistic research about their impact, might close that gap by only one, two, or three points. A dramatic class-size reduction, by almost 30 percent as investigated by at least one study, might creep up to having a five-point impact on that thirty-five-point gap.[23] Far and away the greatest impact we have seen comes from having a highly effective teacher. We know that a top-quartile teacher can close that thirty-five-point achievement gap by around ten points—by roughly one-third—in a single year and that having a top-quartile teacher for four consecutive years could entirely close the gap.[24]

I believe many of the interventions described in this chapter will prove to be powerful levers against the achievement gap if implemented as part of a holistic effort to create the enabling environment for transformational education and build the system's capacity to run transformational schools. Currently, we are measuring not the true power of these interventions but rather their ability to compensate for all the systemic issues that create educational inequity. If we can change the broader construct in which these interventions operate, we are likely to dramatically magnify their impact.

MAKING BIG IDEAS WORK

Each of the ideas and initiatives described in this chapter *can* be important levers in fulfilling the promise of our education system to counter the effects of poverty and level the playing field for all children. Charter school initiatives can work when sufficient attention is focused on vetting incoming proposals, ensuring the necessary leadership and talent, and actually shutting down those schools that are not succeeding. More time in school and reduced class sizes can work when local leadership embraces and invests in these ideas as fundamental, integrated parts of a larger strategy for providing transformational education. Efforts to ensure that every child has highly effective teachers work only alongside other efforts to build transformational, well-run schools. Investing more funding in education, when we first ensure we have the leadership and capacity to spend it well, can of course make a difference.

While pushing one-off solutions outside of the context of comprehensive reform can prove catalytic, the danger is that doing so can send local leaders lurching to fulfill the requirements of a new mandate, rather than empowering them to attain results and enabling them to stay focused on the long, hard work involved in running organizations effectively—recruiting and developing talent, building culture, and managing quality execution. To close the achievement gap, philanthropists and policy makers must be careful to ensure their initiatives will contribute to local capacity-building efforts rather than distracting from them. One important key is to ensure these ideas are pursued in a way that inspires local leadership to assume responsibility for their success as part of their larger agenda. In the previous chapters, we have seen the fundamental role of inspired, committed local leadership with a vision for transformational education and the flexibility to do whatever it takes to achieve results, yet often our policy makers and influencers impose new ideas centrally without taking into account what it will take to ensure their quality execution.

Still, there are bright spots—examples where local leadership and genuine commitment ensured that good, well-intentioned ideas changed outcomes for students. Take the example of small schools. Although, as Bill Gates concluded, that initiative had disappointing results in general, New York City's small schools stand out as a positive exception. Some observers credit the performance of New York City's small schools with helping lift the city's four-year graduation rate by double-digit percentage points over the past five years. One study by the respected research group MDRC (funded by the Gates Foundation) tracked the progress of students randomly assigned to either old large high schools or new smaller ones and found that students in the new small schools were about 7 percent more likely to graduate, which is "roughly one-third the size of the gap in graduation rates between white students and students of color in New York City."[25]

While in many places in the country, the small schools initiative actually amounted to little more than splitting up big high schools, giving each wing a new name and sign, and hiring three more principals to oversee the same staff and structures as before, in New York City Joel Klein had a vision for transformational change and thought deeply about how breaking up the large failing high schools and replacing them with a new generation of small schools could help realize his vision. He viewed the funding provided by the Gates Foundation as an enabler for his vision and sought out a group to be accountable for implementing the reforms and ensuring positive results.

That organization, New Visions for Public Schools, is run by lawyer Robert Hughes, who was an important leader in years of educational equity litigation in the state of New York. Listening to him explain what was involved in the small schools initiative in New York makes abundantly clear that this was nobody's "quick fix" but an all-in commitment of leadership and capacity to ensure that the promise of the smaller schools would be fulfilled. Bob explains that "the mechanics of school creation are a little more complicated than people believe."

He and his organization managed a design competition to create small, intimate schools of no more than four hundred students. "Many proposals lost," he points out. His organization encouraged and demanded that proposals change school structures, set forth a clear vision and rationale for those changes, build in rigorous curricula, establish high expectations for students and children, and track progress on academic goals against clear bench-marks of success. New Visions expected an incoming school team to have a plan for gradually phasing in the new small schools "to ensure that schools established a completely new school culture," Bob says.

In addition, in partnership with the New York Department of Education, New Visions insisted that school design teams were broad and inclusive, composed of civic groups, parents and orga-nizers, community-based organizations, museums, social service agencies, and many others. At the crux of all that work was the in-vestment of on-the-ground leaders with the autonomy to create something new and the responsibility for ensuring it did what it said it would do.

Above all, New Visions wanted to see results. It insisted that schools meet high graduation and attendance targets. "The key was outcomes, outcomes, outcomes," Bob told me. "Like the best schools—charter or district—we wanted the new schools to be or-ganized with a focus on results."

Thus, in New York City, unlike in many places, the small schools initiative was used by Chancellor Klein as a lever to get to all the fundamental elements that he knew were necessary for trans-formational change for students. Both Chancellor Klein and Mayor Bloomberg recognized that the system itself had to change to sup-port changes in schools and wisely threw out strategies that de-manded blind compliance of schools to regulations rather than encouraging innovation to meet student needs. When principals complained of district interference in their efforts to reinvent schools, the department created the Autonomy Zone—a place where schools were given freedom to innovate in exchange for greater accountability for results.

A similar story of the importance of local leadership and com-mitment plays out with another well-intentioned set of policy re-forms that are near and dear to my heart: alternate routes to certification. State laws around the country have enabled school districts to establish these programs to recruit and develop teachers from sources other than schools of education. These laws have enabled Teach For America to work. All our teachers are hired through alternate routes to certification; without their existence we would not be able to place individuals without undergraduate or graduate teacher education as regular teachers. Yet the vast majority of alternate routes to certification have achieved results comparable to those of the traditional teacher education system. An oft-cited study by Mathematica Policy Research and the Institute for Educational Sciences found no difference between alternative certification routes and "regular" certification routes in terms of impact on student achievement.[26]

Alternate routes can have a positive impact on student achievement, but when local leaders don't utilize them as an enabler for transformational change, their implementation falls short. Alternate routes work when school districts and their partners utilize them to recruit talented candidates, select teachers based on high standards, and invest in their training and development. Without this attention to effective execution, we just replicate the system we have.

I've thought a lot about another of the latest policy movements—performance-based pay—from this perspective as well. Anyone who runs schools or school systems recognizes that they would ideally have flexibility in compensating teachers so that they can spend their salary dollars in a way that attracts and retains their highest performers. Yet when systems impose upon principals centrally administered systems that provide small incremental bonuses for teachers who meet centrally determined benchmarks, too often the funding is not spent in the highest-impact ways, and, worse, there are unintended consequences. Without real attention to designing and implementing systems that make sense in the given context, teachers may not even understand why they did or did not receive a bonus. And principals may not be truly able to use the compensation to ensure that the best teachers don't leave; school leaders know, for example, that onetime incremental bonuses are nice but do not change their teachers' career paths by giving them the financial stability to purchase a house, yet so often the centrally designed systems do not account for this.

Policy makers and the business leaders, educators, and philanthropists who advocate for specific reforms simply must formulate their initiatives with an understanding of what it takes to provide transformational education and a respect for the limitations of their own efforts. Central policy making needs to consider how to ensure local leaders are committed to transformational education and provide them with the freedom and support necessary to meet their goals. Otherwise, we run the risk that good ideas won't have their desired effect and, worse, will send local leaders lurching to attract new resources instead of attending to the long, hard work entailed in building strong organizations.

MISPLACING BLAME

In the national discussion on education reform, just as much energy seems to be spent blaming one group or another as lurching from one silver bullet to another. If we could just change parents, or the kids themselves, or educators or their unions, this line of thinking goes, our education woes would be solved. Yet just as the silver-bullet solutions ultimately prove insufficient in solving educational inequity, so too are these silver scapegoats undeserving of all the blame.

Students and Their Families Aren't the Problem

A 2005 Phi Delta Kappa and Gallup poll revealed that the public believes that the three most important factors in creating low educational outcomes in low-income communities are lack of parental involvement, home life and upbringing, and lack of interest on the part of the students themselves. Indeed, not only the general public but many of our most well-read and influential leaders believe that the root of low educational outcomes in urban and rural public schools is a lack of motivation among parents or students; I've sat through many a meeting where people across generations and even representing diverse economic and racial backgrounds express this view. Yet we have seen overwhelming evidence from successful teachers and schools that where children and their families are met with high expectations and a supportive system, they demonstrate intense motivation.

A few years ago, when we asked our corps members whether they felt the general public understands the causes of the achievement gap and its potential solutions, a whopping 98 percent responded that they did not. The consensus of corps members—after they had spent two years working with urban and rural students and their families—was that the public mistakenly blames parents for the achievement gap.

It isn't that our corps members don't believe parents are important. It's that they've found that the vast majority of their students' parents do care and are very responsive to teachers and schools that reach out and show them how to support the educational process. It is only natural that the parents in urban and rural areas, who are less likely themselves to have been successful in school or to have the confidence and know-how to hold teachers and schools to high expectations, will be more likely to be intimidated by the school system and less likely to proactively engage. But the successful teachers and schools described in previous chapters consistently find that good communication and relationship building reveal parent motivation and support. These teachers and schools have also found that in the rare cases where students don't have supportive parents or guardians, it is still possible to succeed. Teachers who embrace the mission of transformational education view that circumstance as one more challenge to overcome—but not as the reason to give up.

It is certainly possible to walk into some classrooms in urban and rural schools and conclude that students aren't motivated. I am certain that I could have walked into another class at Maurice's school when he was teaching there and drawn this conclusion. Yet Maurice's students were some of the hardest-working high school students in the country, which should tell us that the students aren't the issue. Students rise to the occasion when the teacher or school has invested them in working hard—an undertaking all the more important, as we've seen, in communities where there isn't clear and ever-present evidence of the benefits that accrue from academic success.

Seeing students and parents who seem disengaged from the educational process shouldn't lead us to conclude they're the problem. It should lead us to recognize how important it is that teachers and schools adopt a transformational mission and inspire students and families to own it. Indeed, our corps members almost universally report that teachers' own expectations have a much more powerful effect on achievement than any other variable. "Every time I have raised the expectations in my classroom, students have also raised their performance," reported a first grade teacher in Phoenix. "I cannot think of a single student in my classroom who has not had a complete turn-around in behavior, academics, or both because they have been told that they can do it," a teacher from Jefferson Parish in Louisiana said in response to our surveys.

These teachers had similar comments about families' willingness to be involved if given the opportunity. As one seventh grade English and social studies teacher finishing her second year in East Palo Alto put it: "I constantly hear blame being placed on parents who 'just don't care,' and I have found that this is simply not the case. I had parents lined up outside my classroom until 9pm on a conference day that had no earlier notification. Parents are constantly calling me at home or stopping by to check up on their child. The ones who appear to be 'not as involved' have all had very extenuating circumstances (disability, difficult work schedule, etc.). Only a very small percentage 'just don't care.'"

Those who have worked directly with children and families have a different analysis of the role of student and family motivation and engagement than the general public does. Megan Brousseau and Chris Barbic would not cite these factors as the primary barriers to success. When given a purpose and the necessary supports, their students work harder than most students in more privileged circumstances.

"Teachers" Aren't the Problem

Many assume that Teach For America's theory about why we have educational inequity is that today's urban and rural educators don't care as much or aren't as capable as educators in more privileged communities. In fact, this is not our theory. The primary problem isn't that urban and rural teachers and principals are less capable and motivated than they need to be. The primary problem is that our urban and rural educators are asked to tackle much greater challenges than teachers in other communities without receiving the training and professional development to teach or lead in transformational ways, without the management and support to ensure their success, and outside of a context that fosters transformational education.

We have seen that—just as is the case in schools in more privileged communities, and in most organizations for that matter—there is a distribution of effectiveness among teachers in low-income communities. Some urban and rural educators are exceptionally talented and committed. Some could become effective if they received effective training, management, and support and operated within high-performing cultures. Others would be ineffective even if managed and supported differently, whether because they don't work hard enough or don't have the personal characteristics or the academic strength critical to teach effectively. The constant, overgeneralizing discussion about the quality of "teachers" simply has to be demoralizing to hundreds of thousands of individuals who are working hard on behalf of their students.

If we are going to succeed in providing transformational education, one thing is clear: We will need to inspire the deep engagement and leadership of the educators at every level of the system. Instead of blaming them, we should applaud our urban and rural teachers for their commitment to dedicating themselves to tackling the biggest needs in our education system and assume responsibility for the systemic deficiencies that are at work. We should work together with them to change the expectations of teachers and at the same time strengthen our systems for training, managing, supporting, and developing our teachers, and, in cases where it is merited, moving them out of the system.

Teachers' Unions Aren't the Primary Problem, Either

Among school leaders, policy makers, and philanthropists seeking transformational change in America's schools, teachers' unions are a frequent source of frustration and a popular target of blame for lack of progress. Some of the unions' aggressive stances in protecting the interests of their constituents have provided rich fodder for such critiques. Until just recently, there were the infamous "rubber rooms" in New York City where some teachers sat idle, receiving paychecks while waiting for lengthy and incredibly expensive dismissal processes to play out—in the interim costing the city tens of millions of dollars that could have been spent on educating children. Some unions resist collecting and tracking student achievement results in a way that could reveal which teachers are consistently leading students to academic progress and which teachers are not. In some cases unions have resisted the idea that teacher performance should play a role in layoff decisions, forcing children and families to lose some of their most effective teachers (who happen to have the least seniority). Of course, the union's perspective is that these policies have their roots in historical experience that showed school district administrations weren't capable of operating in humane and thoughtful ways—a perspective that is grounded in some truth— though it is difficult to see how these positions have the best interests of kids and educational quality in mind.

Blaming unions for a problem as complex and systemic as this one isn't fair, and it isn't productive, either. It backs groups that we need as allies and partners into a corner, and ultimately, it simply doesn't get us anywhere. What I see and hear as I interact with effective school and district leaders is that—although union contracts and rules need to be reconsidered—massive improvements can be made before we reach the point that collectively bargained regulations constitute the primary impediment to improvement. Often, we focus on the high-hanging fruit and neglect attainable victories.

Ninety-nine percent of all teachers are evaluated as "satisfactory" on teacher evaluation systems—and dismissal rates are at or near zero—whether a district has high union membership or low union membership, or collectively bargained contracts or no contracts.[27] It is hard to argue that unions are *the* reason that we cannot move forward on teacher effectiveness in light of these facts. In fact, teacher dismissals are rare even when teachers do not yet have tenure. A good part of the problem is that whether contracts are collectively bargained or not, school districts have not implemented the type of teacher evaluation systems that are common across high-performing organizations.

We are seeing some signs that unions can be partners in change when embraced as part of the solution. The American Federation of Teachers (AFT) negotiated the landmark teachers' contract in the Washington, D.C., schools that links teacher compensation directly to classroom performance, streamlines dismissal processes for ineffective teachers, and gives principals control over which teachers to hire. In New Haven the AFT codesigned and endorsed a teacher-performance rating system that considers student progress. The AFT recently supported revolutionary legislation in Colorado (discussed in the next chapter) that ties teacher evaluation to student growth, makes it possible to earn and "unearn" tenure based on effectiveness, and makes performance the first factor in layoff decisions. We see in these examples signs that the union can support precisely the sort of systemic changes that we need to ensure that school districts and schools have the capacity and leadership to succeed in a transformational mission.

Although these examples provide reason for optimism, there is clearly so much more to be done. To accomplish a vision of educational excellence and equity, we have no option but to move beyond a blame game and continue seeking to partner with those whose support we'll ultimately need to serve students well. There is much about embracing a transformational mission that has the potential to move us beyond the standoff that has characterized some union negotiations. Committing ourselves to transformational education will require investing more in teacher training and development, officially lengthening the school day and year and paying teachers and administrators more for the longer hours, and improving the quality of school leadership and culture. Even when it comes to accountability, today many unions believe we are asking teachers to accomplish transformational outcomes without truly adopting a transformational mission and providing the support necessary to fulfill it.

Although changing work rules really matters, ultimately when those changes are made we will see how much more we need to do to actually change the way teachers are developed and evaluated. We need to remember that in many of today's schools, teachers are receiving one annual cursory observation, if that. They are often receiving little if any constructive and meaningful feedback and coaching to become more effective. Ultimately, realizing the world we envision will take changes in work rules, but it will take a lot more than that.

CONCLUSION

A front-page article appeared in the *New York Times* in 2010 about the mixed success of charter schools, presenting examples ranging from outright failure to dramatic achievement.[28] The core question posed by the article was, "Why?" What is the key to success in those schools that are outperforming all others—schools where not just a handful but virtually every single student is mastering rigorous content and demonstrating strong reading, writing, math, and thinking skills? Brett Peiser, a leader within the high-performing Uncommon Schools—schools without any of the alluring architecture and technology of the School of the Future—put it simply: "There's not one big thing" that accounts for Uncommon Schools' dramatic success, he said. "There are one hundred one-percent solutions."

Where we see urban and rural children receiving an education that has the potential to change their trajectories, we see leaders who eschew particular "silver bullets" in favor of the hard work of creating an organization with all the elements that are critical to the success of any high-performing institution. The key to success is not one-off mandates around charters, curricula, time in school, funding, and mentor programs. The key to success is local leadership and capacity to employ all the elements of strong vision, culture, accountability, and management that distinguish highly effective organizations.

5

INCREASING THE PACE OF CHANGE

I N THE PAST TWENTY YEARS IN URBAN and rural education reform, we have learned and accomplished a great deal. We have learned that education in low-income communities can and must be transformational—that we can ensure strong outcomes by committing ourselves to changing the trajectory of students from the path their economic background would predict. Not only do we have many more examples of success, but today we have real evidence that replicating success is feasible. And we have begun to understand what it will take to transform whole systems of schools. We are not, however, addressing educational disadvantage at anywhere near the scale of the problem. What will it take to accelerate the pace of change? What must we take on over the next decades to move the needle against the achievement gap? What work, by the next generation of leaders, is going to end educational inequity?

Given that we know that education has the potential to be trans-formative, we must—for the sake of children and families, for our country, and for our collective well-being—do all that it takes to fulfill that potential. More clearly than ever before, we know this requires embracing the principles necessary to achieve ambitious results in any organization, while simultaneously rejecting the distraction of seemingly simpler but ultimately insufficient answers and common excuses.

Today we have a stronger foundation than ever for this work. Because states are developing and adopting ambitious learning standards describing what students across grade levels and subject areas should know and be able to do, we have greater clarity about the educational outcomes we're striving to achieve. And while our assessments must improve in rigor and reliability, we have made significant improvements in our ability to accurately gauge whether students have mastered the content knowledge and critical thinking skills necessary to be prepared for the ensuing academic year and beyond.

Building on this foundation, now we must focus on three priorities that emerge from the lessons we've learned from successful teachers and school leaders and from systems where we are seeing unprecedented positive change. First, we must build the capacity of our education system by building a first-class people-development system. We saw in the first half of this book that "people" emerged as the most central enabling factor in building successful urban and rural schools; on the flip side, conversations with system leaders determined to improve their schools reveal that insufficient access to the "human capital" necessary for success is their greatest constraint. Second, we need to increase the force of policy makers, political leaders, and advocates who understand that transformational education is possible and what it entails, so that we can create the conditions that will enable our educators to be successful and dramatically increase the number of windows of opportunity for the kinds of systemic reforms we are seeing in places like New York, D.C., and New Orleans. Finally, given the magnitude of the problem, we need to foster a new era of innovation in education, to make this work more scalable and more sustainable.

BUILDING AN UNPARALLELED
LEADERSHIP PIPELINE IN EDUCATION

Just about every school and district leader experiencing success in building transformational schools has listed "people" as the number-one priority in his or her work. Consistently, they emphasize the need for a radically different way of thinking about drawing strong and diverse leaders into education and developing them into teachers, principals, and district leaders with the determination and ability to use the power of education to overcome the effects of poverty.

Perhaps five years into Teach For America's history, I spoke to a large group of educators about my belief that school systems should essentially do what Teach For America does—aggressively recruit talent, select teachers based on high standards, and invest in their training and development. One of the people in the audience—a reform-minded leader who had done much to advance the cause of education—was irked. "Why should we have to do this? Accounting firms don't have to do this. Defense contractors don't have to do this."

I suddenly realized the crux of the issue: Too many of our educational leaders don't understand what high-performing organizations in other sectors do to ensure their success. The most effective accounting firms *absolutely* do this; Teach For America competes directly with them for undergraduate business majors on campuses across the country. The most effective defense contractors absolutely do this; we are competing for the same math and science superstars. The most effective law firms are aggressively seeking out (and wining and dining) the very best law students. The top universities are reaching out to the greatest scholars and researchers. The fight for talent is a fundamental element of success in any organization, and there is no reason education should be any different.

I recently had a conversation with Timothy Daly and Ariela Rozman, the president and CEO, respectively, of the New Teacher Project, who have seen numerous examples of school systems' lack of attention to arguably their most valuable resources—their people. When the New Teacher Project first started working with districts in the late 1990s, most human resources departments were approaching teacher hiring with a "we'll take what we can get" attitude. With the view that it was the job of the schools of education to produce the teachers they needed, districts made little effort to search for good candidates and instead minimally screened those who applied. Hiring processes prioritized filling slots quickly rather than identifying teachers with the skills to get results. School systems weren't tracking even the most basic predictive indicators of teacher quality, such as the undergraduate GPAs of their hires. They were investing almost nothing in supporting new teachers to become effective or in evaluating teacher performance. I was always amazed that the human resources officers with whom Teach For America worked almost always reported up to the *operations* team, which focused on processes like payroll and benefits, rather than reporting to the executives in the district responsible for academic results. Today, there are some promising developments in this arena, but we are still far from where we need to be.

The failure to prioritize human capital is what led to a situation in which Philadelphia's School of the Future, arguably a setting so unique that it deserved careful matching of teachers with unique skills, was not staffed until a few weeks before school opened. The hiring process involved hastily choosing teachers from other schools in the system who were looking for reassignment—not from an aggressive search for people who would fit the school's particular needs or were drawn to its unique vision and values.

Tim Daly recalled one time when he visited another school's office, only days before a newly hired principal was to take over, and observed district human resources staff in the principal's office filling empty classrooms with teachers who had been refused by all the other schools in the district. When the new principal arrived, the human resources staff told her they had done her a favor by staffing her school. In reality, they had hidden their problematic employees in a school that couldn't raise a protest. No highly functioning organization in any sector—from Johns Hopkins Hospital to Apple Computer, from the U.S. Marines to General Electric—would operate with such disregard for identifying and choosing staff members. And as we have seen, no highly functioning organization in education does, either.

The Widget Effect, an influential study that Tim led at the New Teacher Project, brought to light the myriad ways that districts treat all teachers as if they are interchangeable. Districts, the study found, "fail to distinguish great teaching from good, good from fair, and fair from poor. A teacher's effectiveness—the most important factor for schools in improving student achievement—is not measured, recorded, or used to inform decision-making in any meaningful way."[1] Considering every stage of the people-development continuum—recruitment, hiring and placement, professional development, compensation, granting tenure, retention, layoffs, remediation, and dismissal—the study found that teacher performance was taken into account *only* at the remediation and dismissal stages. Even then, at least half the districts studied had not dismissed a single experienced teacher for poor performance in the previous five years. Just as problematic, the report found that high-performing teachers were rarely celebrated.

Happily, we do see more and more districts taking on the hard fight to find, develop, and keep strong leaders in classrooms and schools. Whereas ten years ago virtually no district had anyone in charge of developing a comprehensive strategy for building a high-quality workforce, today a number of districts organize themselves with a strong focus on people. These districts are experiencing real success in attracting strong talent to their teaching positions—debunking the myth that this is impossible given the image and status of teaching. Several districts have partnered with the New Teacher Project to establish "Teaching Fellows" programs that attract midcareer professionals to the classroom through aggressive recruitment and marketing strategies that challenge prospective teachers to take action against education inequity. Candidates are carefully selected based on high standards, placed as full-time teachers, and credentialed through alternate routes to certification. The Teaching Fellows programs are proving in communities across the country that qualified, diverse individuals jump at the chance to teach when recruited effectively.

In 2010 in New York City, for example, more than 10,000 individuals applied to the Teaching Fellows, and only 8 percent were admitted based on the personal characteristics the district believes to be predictive of success. Fellows' average undergraduate GPA was 3.3, and 23 percent came into the program with one advanced degree.[2] Moreover, 37 percent of the 2010 cohort is African American or Latino, compared to 12 percent of all teachers nationwide.[3] A 2007 study by the Urban Institute found that through the Teaching Fellows program and Teach For America, New York City had considerably narrowed the teacher-qualification gaps in low-income versus high-income schools (based on categories such as SAT scores, selectivity of undergraduate program, and first-attempt pass rates on the teacher certification exam).[4] Tim described the evolution that the New Teacher Project has observed in districts during its consultations with them. First came an emerging emphasis on pro-actively recruiting and selecting individuals with the personal characteristics deemed necessary to succeed. Next came a greater emphasis on how to attract high-potential educators to the schools that had historically received less than a fair share of talent. Now some districts are beginning to pay more attention to how well those people are performing in their roles, providing rewards and support where warranted to ensure that our best teachers are retained for the long haul. We are headed in the right direction, but much more remains to be done.

Adopting a "Talent Mindset"

Imagine how different the education sector would look if we adopted a "talent mindset." This is a phrase popularized by the best-selling book *The War for Talent*, which put forth the notion that the most valuable resource in today's world is talent. The book asserts that managers and leaders need to adopt the belief that increasing the caliber of their workforce is their responsibility, and, moreover, it is the most important factor contributing to their success. Jim Collins, who has spent his career studying the distinguishing characteristics of highly effective business and social-sector organizations, makes the same point in his influential book, *Good to Great*: "The old adage 'People are your most important asset' turns out to be wrong. People are not your most important asset. The *right* people are." His studies of organizations revealed that those that rose above the crowd and became great were the ones that "got the right people on the bus, the wrong people off the bus, and then the right people in the right seats." To be clear, as Jim Collins emphasizes, this intense focus on finding and developing great people is not a "business" idea; it is an "excellence" idea that plays out across all types of organizations, from hospitals and sports teams to nonprofits and schools.[5]

With a talent mindset, school systems would aggressively recruit—*actually go out and find*—exceptionally talented people with leadership potential, encouraging them to take positions as teachers. They would not be sitting back, waiting to see who comes to them. Data from the National Center for Education Statistics revealed that in 2007–2008, teachers were twice as likely to have graduated from the bottom tier of higher-education institutions based on selectivity than the top tier.[6] And as Arthur Levine, former president of Columbia University's Teachers College, pointed out in his 2006 report on teacher education programs, aspiring elementary school teachers had considerably lower scores on the SAT and Graduate Record Examination than the national average.[7] While Teach For America has found in its own research that academic performance alone is not the path to great teaching, nonetheless we can all agree that teachers should not come, on average, from among the least academically accomplished. This means that school systems should recruit aggressively at schools of education to attract the strongest candidates, and they should also recruit as far beyond them as necessary to find as many candidates of the caliber and diversity as they need.

With a talent mindset, school systems would also insist on ownership of the development of their teachers since districts are held accountable for the teachers' results and also have the best understanding of what teachers need to do to ensure students' success. As we learned in Chapter 2, this is what KIPP, Uncommon Schools, and Achievement First are doing with the creation of Teacher U at Hunter College—which is going to award master's degrees based not on courses taken but on proven effectiveness in the classroom. School systems might choose to contract out the development of their talent, but they would be contracting for performance, not bodies. They would insist on knowing (as they now do in Louisiana) each teacher-preparation partner's record of producing effective teachers.

This would be a radically different education world. Schools and school systems would be training principals and school-level teams to act on all the principles of effective management and support—ensuring that teachers have clear goals and that they reflect regularly on what more they can do to reach those goals, and providing coaching and professional development tailored to each individual teacher's developmental needs. School and system leaders would make it their number-one priority to know which of their employees are most effective and would work to keep those people, enticing them with additional responsibility, autonomy, recognition, and compensation. Districts would lay out clear and compelling career paths that would enable successful teachers to remain in the classroom while gaining more influence over time and also to move into positions of school and system leadership. As these leaders move through the organization, taking on more responsibility in each new role, they would receive the training and development necessary to succeed at each leadership stage.

In education we often talk about "teacher quality" and "principal quality" as if they are two distinctly different things. Yet as Dacia Toll, Norman Atkins, and the leaders of other high-performing charter networks tell us in Chapter 2, they are in fact closely related. Of course, not every successful teacher would make a successful principal, as the purview of a principal extends beyond ensuring student achievement. But successful teaching is the foundational experience for great educational leadership. Extraordinary classroom success provides school leaders with conviction in what is possible, shapes insights about effective teaching that inform effective teacher selection and development, and conveys the moral authority to insist on nothing less than exceptional results. Indeed, just about every school I've seen that is producing transformational results for students—including all those I have described in this book—is run by someone who started off as an extremely successful teacher.

In the cases where teachers are not performing well and not likely to improve, principals with a talent mindset would make the decision to remove that teacher from the organization—the same way a manager would decide to terminate an ineffective employee in any other highly effective organization. Where union regulations are an impediment to moving ineffective people out, districts would be making specific proposals for better processes that protect students from poor teaching while also protecting teacher rights. Certainly, we can understand why teachers who are often lucky to get one observation a year—and even luckier when that observation is followed by meaningful feedback—would be anxious about giving principals more freedom over dismissals. In many cases, district management and labor would have to step back to create a new system for teacher development and evaluation that better serves both students and their teachers.

To increase the pace of change, we must prioritize the hard work of building a strong leadership pipeline. While there seems to be a growing recognition among state and local policy makers about the importance of "human capital," we must not let that recognition translate into yet another round of "quick-fix" mandates on school districts that do not have the capacity to effectively implement them. Strategies like better mentoring programs, career ladders, or performance pay could be critical elements of a "talent mindset" approach in any given school system, but we will need to resist the temptation to mandate them at the state or federal level. Unless these strategies are implemented as part of a coherent vision for the people-development systems necessary to support transformational education, they will only become part of the list of one-off solutions that have little or no effect. Building the strong leadership pipeline that we need is going to require building district capacity, not top-down mandates.

Establishing Internal Learning Cycles

Much of what needs to happen is at the school level, where principals must develop the capacity to recruit, select, and develop their teams far more effectively than they currently do. At the same time, it is also important for school systems to better support their schools in this regard. One crucial step is to capture information and develop knowledge about what differentiates effective teachers and leaders and how to select, train, and develop more of them.

This is an area where Teach For America's experience in recruiting and developing corps members can be instructive. "The fundamental starting point is creating a closed loop of information so that you can evaluate your decisions and choices and increase the effectiveness of your people," says my colleague Matt Kramer, who is Teach For America's president and one of the best thinkers I've met on this topic. Matt joined us from McKinsey and Company, a management consulting firm where, among other roles, he consulted with the New York City Department of Education as well as with Teach For America. Matt helped us build those learning loops within our organization. "So you start off with things you know about a person when you hire them," he explains. "Then you take note of the things you do with them to help them succeed. And then you gather information about the extent to which they're successful. Once you have that system for managing information in place, you can use your outcomes to better inform your strategies. You have to have a full connection between the things you do and whether they work—that's a foundational element of an effective organization."

This learning cycle, critical for organizations in general, is an essential underpinning of effective people-development systems. It enables a district or school to ask itself: Of all the many investments we are making in our people, from how we select them to how we support them, what is working and what is not? What investments are paying dividends in the form of student learning? As Matt describes, "Based on what you are learning, you create real clarity for people to know what they need to do to be successful. When you have theories, you test them out, and you usually evolve your thinking. That cycle is the beginning of everything."

These considerations are at the heart of what Michelle Rhee and Jason Kamras have infused into the D.C. public school system. "Number one, you need some basic reliable data on performance to inform all the other decisions on the human capital front," Jason told me. "You have to have that transparency to know where your best recruitment pipelines are, how your selection of teachers is and is not working, how to make smart tenure and promotional decisions, how to target retention efforts strategically. We have to know who is most and least effective based on fair and objective metrics in order to make good decisions and get better as a system."

At Teach For America, we have made a considerable long-term investment in staffing and resources to drive this learning for our own organization. Every year, for example, we review our teachers' student achievement data and compare it to the information we had gathered on them in the admissions process; this allows us to refine our understanding of the best predictors of teacher effectiveness. How predictive of student learning is a candidate's GPA, for example? (It turns out that although cumulative GPA is somewhat predictive, GPA in the later college years is more predictive than GPA from earlier years. Factoring this into an applicant's evaluation significantly improves the predictive value of his or her GPA.) How predictive is prior experience in a low-income community? (Based on early results, we didn't find predictiveness. But with further study, we've found that certain types of experiences may predict success.) What aspects of a candidate's experience, dispositions, skills, and knowledge are most predictive of student learning in their classroom? These evolving findings have helped us improve our selection model every year.

We have built the same sort of learning loop into our training and support system. When we have teachers showing dramatic student progress, we want to know what they are doing differently from other teachers. What can we learn from our most effective teachers' strategies that can be used to improve the effectiveness of our moderately effective and struggling teachers? This is, in essence, the learning I described in our visits to the classrooms of Megan, Maurice, and Priscilla in the first chapter of this book. We are identifying patterns in how successful teachers approach their work that inform how we train and support the next incoming group of corps members.

We also want to know which aspects of our training program contribute to corps member success. What impact will a particular online course in math-content pedagogy have on new teachers' actions and their students' achievement? (The preliminary results of this pilot are strong, and we are now testing it with more of our math teachers.) What form of teacher resource dissemination has the best chance of actually impacting our teachers' classroom actions? (We are finding that support tools and resources shared one-on-one by our teacher coaches—"program directors" who each support about thirty-five corps members—represent one of our best means of influencing teacher performance.)

When districts set out to learn from Teach For America, they often ask what our specific admissions criteria are, or whether they can adopt our Teaching As Leadership rubric that captures our current hypotheses about what teacher actions most correlate with dramatic student achievement. These might be helpful starting points, but what districts really need to do is invest in their own learning loops. Participating in the process generates better context-specific insights and builds investment in the information it yields, investment that is crucial to successful execution over time.

Increasing the Diversity of the Talent Pipeline

We have seen at Teach For America that our most effective corps members—those who have effected the greatest academic progress— represent all races, ethnicities, and socioeconomic backgrounds. We have also seen that when such teachers are themselves from racial and economic backgrounds similar to those of the students they teach, they have the potential to make a profound additional impact; they can be particularly persuasive with students by their example as well as through their words regarding the connection between academic achievement and success in life. They may also be partic-ularly qualified to serve as counselors for students who are grappling with the tensions involved in the pursuit of academic success— students who might face extra challenges in their efforts or might fear that their academic success will result in leaving their commu-nity behind or in becoming disconnected from their peers. Of course, the potential for additional impact must not lull teachers who share the racial, ethnic, or economic backgrounds of their stu-dents into relying on such commonalities and underinvesting in the incredibly hard work it takes to become a great teacher. But given the additional value that people who share the backgrounds of their students can have, we—Teach For America and the education sector as a whole—have to redouble our efforts to ensure that people of diverse racial and economic backgrounds are well represented in the leadership pipeline we are building.

This is a particularly challenging imperative given that the very problem of educational inequity is itself played out on college campuses where teaching careers are often launched. At the 340 most selective public and private colleges in the country, only 5 percent of graduates are African American and 6 percent are Latino; 17 percent are from low-income backgrounds.[8] Teach For America actively recruits at these and many more schools; contrary to popular perception, we don't just focus on the historically elite schools, and our admissions model doesn't give any special weighting to applicants from those schools. Our aggressive recruiting efforts have allowed Teach For America to attract African American and Latino applicants at a rate that is disproportionate to their representation among the senior class at the most selective institutions. In 2010, 32 percent of incoming corps members identify as people of color, including 11 percent who identify as African American and 7 percent who identify as Latino. Twenty-eight percent received Pell grants, and 20 percent are the first in their families to attend college. There's a lot more we must do, however, before we achieve the levels of diversity that would be optimal, and we recognize that we—and the entire education sector— have much more to do to ensure that more of our nation's leaders of color, and leaders from low-income communities, are channeling their skills and insights toward solving the problem of educational inequity.

○ ○ ○

WHEN WE LOOK CAREFULLY at the growing number of successful and improving classrooms, campuses, and school systems serving low-income children, we see that strong leadership—people with uncompromising vision for student success, the ability to inspire others to share that vision, and the courage and perseverance to do whatever it takes to put children on a different path in life—is the nonnegotiable catalyst for meaningful change. For too long, the education sector has been too passive in its approach to finding, selecting, and developing these leaders. It is possible to create a leadership pipeline in education that successfully competes for our nation's top talent, but we have to think differently about the sorts of investments necessary to create that pipeline. By scaling up what is working in pockets across the country, we can build a diverse, high-caliber force of highly effective leaders in classrooms, schools, and school systems.

FOSTERING EFFECTIVE POLITICAL LEADERSHIP AND ADVOCACY

In previous chapters we have seen the role policy change has played in empowering educators to effect transformational results. The progress in New Orleans, Washington, D.C., and New York City was enabled by unprecedented governance change. The challenge going forward is not just to seize those opportunities that become available because an entire system fails but to proactively create many more such opportunities.

For years, well-intentioned policy makers have operated from the assumption that serving children and families well necessitated safeguarding children's interests through policy mandates and process requirements. Our education policies are therefore for the most part a patchwork of top-down requirements that aim to mandate all the actions that educators must take. Yet everything we have learned—from the high-performing charter school management organizations and from improving school systems—makes it impossible to imagine that we will attain results that are meaningful for students and families through efforts to micromanage the people in the system. Replicating transformational education requires empowering educators to do what is right for students while holding them accountable for results. It will also take other policy changes that foster the development of first-class people-development systems, for example, or make it possible to lengthen the school day and year. In some states, it will require greater financial investment. We don't want these initiatives to become the next silver bullets, and so they will need to be designed in a way that empowers local leadership rather than distracting from the work of building strong local organizations.

At the federal level, sweeping policy changes have created a context that is accelerating the kinds of changes we need. The No Child Left Behind Act, for all its flaws and the controversies it ignited, reset the national conversation about education, especially regarding the vast gap in outcomes between students in low- and higher-income neighborhoods. The true magnitude of the achievement gap in America was, for decades, unclear, as most of our attention focused on inequitable inputs (e.g., dollars, or numbers of books in libraries) rather than outputs (how much students are actually learning). Aspiring to raise the quality of education for all students through a call for standards, assessments, and accountability, the 2002 law called for annual improvements in student performance and set forth penalties for districts that did not achieve those improvements.

This law shifted the conversation about education in our school districts, focusing our attention on students' demonstrable academic achievement. With its bipartisan embrace of accountability and high expectations, NCLB fostered an environment that valued the results-oriented, achievement-driven leadership that we see at the helm of virtually every high-performing or quickly improving classroom, school, and district in the country.

We also saw in the years following NCLB, however, that it isn't possible for a national initiative to effect significant progress without inspiring the commitment of local leadership. Many states responded to NCLB by watering down standards and assessments, in essence making the tests easier in order to make results look better.

An *Education Sector* report found widespread exaggeration of improvement in areas such as student performance, graduation rates, teacher qualifications, and school safety. According to that report, "For every measure, the pattern was the same: a significant number of states used their standard-setting flexibility to inflate the progress that their schools are making and thus minimize the number of schools facing scrutiny under the law."[9] (Of course, this is exactly the response that leads policy makers to respond with more central mandates, leading to a vicious cycle.)

In 2010 President Obama's "Race to the Top" initiative sought deeper local- and state-level commitment to change. The Obama administration made available $4.3 billion in grants to states where all the parties—states, districts, unions, nonprofits—come together to embrace the principles that we've seen work in improving school systems. To receive funding, states had to put forth compelling plans embracing a common set of standards for what children should know and be able to do at each grade level in each subject across the country, commiting to invest in data systems that will enable the development of learning loops at every level, promoting human capital reform to ensure we are attracting and developing the necessary teaching and leadership talent, and focusing particularly on turning around the most underperforming of our schools.

Even in this national context, it will be a challenge to move to a policy environment that provides educators with the support necessary to provide transformational education without the unintended consequences of centrally mandating one-off "solutions" that lack their buy-in. From what we have seen, it seems that the most promising path is to generate more political leaders, advocates, and union leaders who deeply understand that educational inequity is a solvable problem, who appreciate what solving the problem will take, and who have the conviction to stand up for the change that is necessary.

Coalitions for Change

In recent years, we have seen new collaborations and initiatives that might have seemed unthinkable a few years ago. In 2009 Michael Johnston, whose convictions about the potential of children in low-income communities were in part developed as a Teach For America corps member in the Mississippi Delta in 1997, was appointed to the Colorado Senate at the young age of thirty-four when the seat was vacated. Before his appointment to the senate, Michael was a founding leader of a high school, where the majority of students qualified for free and reduced lunch, that moved its college acceptance rate from 50 percent to 100 percent—every one of his graduating students was admitted to a four-year college. Michael was inspired by his students' hard work and accomplishments, and he wanted to clear the way for more classroom and school leaders to achieve similar results.

A Democrat, Michael joined forces with a Republican to cosponsor legislation that would make changes that are foundational for districts to develop strong leadership pipelines and for empowering school principals to develop the teaching forces necessary to run transformational schools. The bill, passed a few months later, ties teacher evaluation and tenure to the academic progress of their students, holds principals accountable for student achievement and teacher development, ends the practice of forcing principals to hire teachers against their will, and releases districts from old "last hired, first fired" rules in case of layoffs. In an editorial, Michael and his cosponsor explained that "research confirms that the two most important school-based factors in improving student achievement are the effectiveness of the teacher and the principal. . . . Yet, we still don't have an agreed-upon definition of a great teacher or principal. Our bill starts that process by requiring that definitions of teacher and principal effectiveness depend on how well their students are growing."[10]

Michael was able to build a broad coalition of supporters that included advocacy groups like Stand for Children and Jóvenes y Padres Unidos, as well as a broad coalition of civil rights groups, business organizations, and labor (the American Federation of Teachers signed on in support, though the National Education Association opposed it). Even with this broad coalition, passage of this bill was a difficult battle. The debates over teachers' responsibility for students' success or failure created new fissures between traditional political allies. Teachers, unions, and political leaders lined up on both sides of the issues. The debate reached a low when one Democratic representative who was arguing against evaluating teachers based on student performance said on the floor of the state capitol, "Well, if you were running a business baking bread and the flour came in to you full of maggots and worms and you had to use it . . . you would not be able to produce a good product, would you?"[11] In a number of ways, the intensity of the disagreements and the tensions between adult and student interests sparked by the proposed legislation demonstrated just how critical it is to have political leaders who have acquired unshakable conviction through firsthand understanding of the potential of children in under-resourced areas.

The passage of this bill highlights the need for sophisticated political advocacy on behalf of children and for broad-based coalition building to break out of the entrenched policies that protect the broken status quo. In addition to Michael's and others' leadership on the issues, this bill needed advocates with in-depth knowledge of the legislative process to influence when and how hearings were framed, to keep important polling data in front of key legislators, to gather and present supportive signatures, and to manage the testimony of dozens of supporters of the bill.

The passage of this bill is, on the one hand, a hopeful indicator of what is possible when political savvy and coalition building are applied to transforming our education system. On the other hand, it is a reminder of just how far we are from having the political leadership and advocacy infrastructure to effect these sorts of changes all across the country. We need hundreds more victories like this one to move our country in the right direction.

A New Generation of Political Leaders

Michael provides a vivid example of the kind of political leadership we need to create a context conducive to progress. His understanding of the drivers of transformational education, his unwavering conviction about the importance of effecting significant change, and his ability to develop a diverse coalition to support contentious changes enabled him to pioneer legislation that inspired the current and three former governors of Colorado to state in an editorial that "no proposal has greater promise for transforming education in Colorado."[12]

We must create a much larger community of political leaders — on both sides of the aisle and at all levels of government — who understand the stakes, what is possible, and what it takes to win the fight against educational inequity. While we have the potential to grow that political community by ensuring our future leaders have been successful teachers in low-income areas, just as Michael Johnston was, we have considerable work ahead of us to encourage and support people with the necessary conviction and courage on education issues to run for office. In the tradition of the most aggressive political action committees in the country (entities more often associated with narrow special interests), we must create powerful organizations that shape, choose, and support candidates with the most potential.

Democrats for Education Reform offers a relatively new example of this model. Led by former award-winning education journalist Joe Williams, Democrats for Education Reform bundles resources and support for local and national candidates who are willing to stand up for reforming education. Sometimes those stances challenge entrenched interests within the Democratic Party, and this organization offers political backing for challenging the status quo.

Teach For America cannot and should not be the primary source of such leaders, though I am confident that it will be a key contributor as more and more of our alumni accept the call to serve in public office. We are restricted in our political engagement activity, but a separate organization called Leadership for Educational Equity (LEE) engages our alumni in this work. LEE, a 501(c)4, provides direct resources, opportunities, and support for our alumni who, irrespective of party affiliation, are interested in participating in politics, policy, and advocacy.

One person LEE has supported in his efforts to exert political influence is Carl Zaragoza, who joined Teach For America after serving in the army. He taught eighth grade social studies in Phoenix. Carl was assigned the lowest-performing students in the school, and many of them were reading at a third grade level. With hard work and with methods that often chafed against conventional practice—he was reprimanded for giving students' families his phone number and was required to end his practice of visiting students' homes—Carl was able to improve his students' literacy skills by about two grade levels in just nine months. His students demonstrated mastery of the state-mandated content objectives for social studies.

At the end of his two-year commitment to Teach For America, as Carl was deciding whether to stay in the classroom, his principal informed him that social studies courses at the school would be discontinued. Carl was told that if he really wanted to return, they would see if they could find a math or science placement for him, but Carl says it was clear he was not being asked to come back.

Uncertain about his next career move, Carl began bartending. He was quickly promoted and was soon managing a chain of restaurants in the Phoenix area. But, as Carl says, "I was always thinking and talking about my kids and education."

When his school district was declared to be "failing" by the state, Carl decided to attend the school board meeting to see if he could help address the problems. The entire school board meeting, however, was dedicated to "redoing the math," Carl says. The school board members just kept running numbers, cutting out various groups of kids, and then "they actually celebrated that if you look at the data this way instead of the way the state did, we're in the second to worst category, not the worst category." Carl recalls, "They saw it as a math game. It was just unbelievable."

Thinking about his own students, Carl decided he would run for a seat on the school board. He took his incredulity to the voters. He describes his platform simply: "All kids can learn, and excuses are unacceptable." The issue as he saw it wasn't so much teacher quality as lack of leadership and accountability. Carl won the election (in which about 20,000 votes were cast) by 26 votes.

He inadvertently rocked the boat at the very first meeting. The school board had a tradition of electing its president more or less by consensus. Carl broke that tradition by asking if other members could talk about their vision for the school board's role and the district's future, so that he could make an informed decision on whom to support.

The other board members were outraged, but Carl was undeterred. He had prepared ten questions about the direction of the district that he thought would help clarify everyone's vision. How are teachers evaluated? What are the accountability structures? His colleagues would not answer the questions, so Carl put his own hat into the ring to run for president and answered those ten questions himself. The other board members all voted against him in his bid.

Carl has continued to rock the boat, visiting all the schools in the district, building relationships with teachers and administrators and listening to their concerns, and insisting the district focus on what is working and what is not. After a couple of years of consistently asking the same fundamental questions about what the district is doing to impact student achievement, the core business of the school board has dramatically changed. "When I began," he said, "most of the conversations—really, most of the conversations—were about copy machines and contracts and stuff like that. Today, that's changed. Now, every meeting is about what we as a district are doing to increase student learning. That's the focus. And now we have seven of our nine campuses improved to 'performing-plus' status. Reading growth has quadrupled the state average. We should celebrate this growth, and I think teachers are feeling proud. It's working. We just cannot argue with the results."

Carl is a prime example of the sort of political leadership that will be required at every level of the system over the coming decades. We need political leaders on school boards, in state legislatures, and in the nation's capitol whose perspectives are informed by understanding what is driving results in the successful classrooms and schools, and improving districts, across the country.

Building State and Local Advocacy Infrastructure

Even as we work to increase the number of political leaders like Michael and Carl, we must expand the advocacy infrastructure necessary to amplify the influence of those who know what is possible in urban and rural education. I have personally experienced the impact of effective advocacy in Connecticut. Dacia Toll, who was working to create a teacher and principal pipeline for the Achievement First schools, asked that we consider developing a Teach For America site there since she viewed our presence as important to the growth of her network.

Unfortunately, various policy barriers made expanding to Connecticut a tricky proposition. Unlike in other states, Connecticut laws made it impossible, for example, for our corps members to get certified while they were teaching. (Teach For America corps members are able to teach in regions with alternate certification paths that enable individuals without traditional teacher education degrees to teach while working toward certification.) As a national organization without strong knowledge of and connections to the political landscape in Connecticut, this represented a real barrier to our work in that state.

Thankfully, there was a highly effective Connecticut-based advocacy organization called the Connecticut Coalition for Achievement Now (ConnCAN) that teamed with key champions in the state legislature to garner support for our cause. ConnCAN's mission is to reform Connecticut's public schools by building a movement of concerned citizens who advocate for smart public policies in the state's educational system. Led in partnership by CEO Alex Johnston and COO Marc Porter Magee, ConnCAN helped push legislation through the state legislature that enabled our initial corps members in Connecticut to teach on short-term certification permits. This was a critical stopgap solution for us while we pursued longer-term strategies for addressing our certification challenges in the state. (Today, based on the demonstrated effectiveness of our training and support program, we are able to certify our own teachers in Connecticut.)

Each year ConnCAN runs coordinated campaigns to pass reforms that improve outcomes. In our four years in Connecticut, we have watched ConnCAN deftly mobilize highly influential civic leaders as well as traditionally underrepresented families in low-income communities where children have the most to gain and lose from state and local education policies. For example, when much-needed legislation to make student achievement data public and transparent seemed to be dying on the vine in a polarized state legislature, ConnCAN activated its 15,000 members and flooded politicians with e-mails insisting the bill get passed. It did. On another occasion, a politically popular bill that contained several items of legislation key to the education reform movement in Connecticut, including a new teaching certificate that was critical to Teach For America's future in the state, was quashed by an unrelated political tiff on the last day of the legislature's session. The next morning, ConnCAN unleashed a torrent of dissatisfaction from its members, giving the bill's legislative supporters the opportunity to resurrect it and pass it into law during a special session. As I was writing this book, ConnCAN had achieved three major legislative victories through its most recent "Mind the Gaps" campaign: overhauling the state's teacher certification rules, opening up scores of longitudinal student achievement data to the public, and securing $20 million of funding for the expansion of high-performing public charter schools despite an $8 billion state budget deficit.

Unfortunately, few communities have organizations that combine an understanding of what works for kids in underresourced communities with the political savvy to influence local and state governments to act. The closest thing to ConnCAN I have found elsewhere is the formidable political influence of Leslie Jacobs in New Orleans. While many people think of Katrina as the "reason" New Orleans schools turned around, the foundations for change had started forming much earlier; the storm actually accelerated changes already being made. As we saw in Chapter 3, Leslie Jacobs, the "bulldog of education,"[13] had readied the state legislature to take bold action. She was sounding the alarm from her role on the state board of education and through her close connections to legislators and governors, creating a landscape in which the community was demanding change. Leslie has now founded her own organization—Educate Now!—that is singularly dedicated to ensuring that decisions are made to increase student opportunities. Educate Now! provides constantly updated information on student progress in New Orleans, both the good and the bad news, as well as programmatic support to the various reforms playing out in New Orleans.

To start to close the achievement gap in America, we will need dozens more organizations like Stand for Children, which played an important role in the changes described above in Colorado, ConnCAN, and Educate Now! We need, at the local level, the sort of single-minded and politically savvy advocacy for children that Kati Haycock's Education Trust provides nationally—exposing the magnitude of educational inequity, showing the possibility of success, and shaping legislation, all in the dogged pursuit of educational excellence for all children. What's particularly promising about what these on-the-ground advocacy organizations are doing is that they are catalyzing advocacy within and from the community itself. By insisting that the community be informed not only about the effectiveness of their schools but also about the avenues for influencing their schools, organizations like these are working to ensure the movement for educational equity is diverse and representative of the community's interests. The path from our current world, where we can list the limited examples of effective policy change, to the world we need, where these examples are too many to count and are generating windows of opportunity across local, state, and federal levels, involves developing in many more young and established leaders the conviction that educational disadvantage is a problem than can in fact be solved, the understanding of how to solve it, and the political skills necessary to marshal community support and effectively navigate the legislative process.

INNOVATION TO CHANGE THE TRAJECTORY OF REFORM

Right now, it seems that in education we do everything the hardest possible way. If we can do something by hand, we do it by hand. Take, for example, the situation Michelle Rhee found in 2007 when she arrived in Washington, D.C.: millions of disorganized personnel files and no electronic records, no e-mail system through which the school system could communicate directly with all teachers and other employees, and only the most rudimentary means of collating and analyzing data from classrooms and schools to see where progress was and was not being made. This was not such an exceptional situation. Tim Daly from The New Teacher Project told me that nine of the twelve districts studied in *The Widget Effect* in 2009 still had paper personnel records. Today, the vast majority of classrooms I enter are organized in the same structure (one teacher and thirty kids), with teachers employing the same technology (maybe an overhead projector) as classrooms decades ago.

Our education systems—like institutions in virtually ever other sector—need to find ways to be dramatically more effective and efficient. Given how much remains to be done and how difficult this work is, we simply have to leverage every tool at our disposal to make our efforts more productive and sustainable. Imagine how different our work would be if all of us—parents, children, and teachers—were actually able to see and follow students' learning and growth. That world is well within reach, given today's technology. We have seen in our most effective classrooms the powerful effect of enabling students to track their own progress. Right now—and this is true in both rich and poor neighborhoods—parents and kids generally have no idea where they are in relation to the expected standards of learning and mastery. Making this information accessible could realign the pressures and supports around students and schools. It might also help lead to a world where the community is protesting against districts for keeping failing schools open instead of protesting against districts for closing them.

Our best teachers often say, at least early on in their careers, that they are great culture builders but not great "teachers"—meaning they are good at setting a vision and motivating students to work toward it but are not yet experts at teaching any given concept in the most efficient and effective way possible. Imagine the tools we could provide teachers to help them help students understand material. Given how captivated students are by computer games, shouldn't we be taking advantage of that technology to help them advance their skills in math, science, and even reading?

I myself saw the potential power of this approach when one of our supporters asked me to test out a new educational software program with my oldest son Benjamin, who was four and a half. He hadn't shown any inclination to read, yet after two months of obsessively using this computer program, he was reading and comprehending at a second grade level. Although every kid won't respond in the same way to any given educational intervention (and this particular program was less of a fixation for my other sons), we simply must experiment with software that can advance the learning of children as well as form the foundation for a transformation of our educational infrastructure.

Certainly, we risk overdependence on computers and online learning when our children also need to be developing social and interactive skills. And as we've seen in earlier chapters, technology will not be effective if schools lack motivational missions, leaders, and teachers. What's so compelling about the growing number of successful uses of computer-learning technology, though, is the power of these tools to actually differentiate instruction. In a traditional classroom, where one teacher is working with twenty, thirty, or even forty children, it's exceedingly difficult to target each child's academic strengths and needs. The more sophisticated technology-enabled learning models are doing just that. Software is able to diagnose and keep track of a child's progress on dozens of learning objectives, quickly moving on from concepts the child has mastered and offering additional practice in the areas where the child needs help.

Others are innovating around the theme of differentiating instruction in actual classroom design. A pilot program in New York City called the School of One is challenging the one-size-fits-all model of one teacher instructing dozens of children. Launched by Joel Rose, a Teach For America alumnus and former chief executive of human capital for New York City's Department of Education, the School of One gives each student a daily customized schedule (called a "play list") that incorporates a variety of learning modalities: one-on-one tutoring, small-group collaboration, traditional teacher-delivered lessons, and technology-based instruction. At the end of each day, students complete an assessment; their daily achievement data is then coupled with information about the students' known learning preferences and a snapshot of available classroom resources to provide personalized student schedules for the next day. In addition to differentiating instruction for every student, the School of One optimizes the value and utility of its teachers. In the conventional model, a teacher is responsible for teaching all grade- and subject-specific content to all students over the course of the year. At the School of One, teachers are responsible for a specific subset of content, perhaps teaching a set of lessons to various groups of students at different points during the year. Technology is leveraged to teach concepts that are best conveyed in a visual and dynamic way, while teachers are freed up to focus on individual student needs or particular student misconceptions as well as on higher-order skills like synthesizing and analyzing.

Another innovative and promising model is Rocketship Schools, which—in addition to pursuing the mission and strategies for people development and culture building that distinguish other highly successful schools—uses state-of-the-art online learning systems to differentiate instruction for students on basic skills. The still evolving hybrid software/instructor model saves teacher time and money and allows teachers to focus on higher-order objectives with students. Rocketship's flagship schools in San Jose, California, in their first and second years of existence, have already risen to the top of the rankings of academically successful low-income elementary schools across California. The network is now poised to grow rapidly and bring its low-cost, high-performing model to dozens of communities across the country.

There seems to be immense potential in technology to improve education, but we need to think beyond technological solutions to provide our children with better, as well as more efficient, education. The space for innovating in education, with technology, school design, training systems, and so forth, is wide open. A small number of highly effective schools, for example, are experimenting with purposefully bringing together children from high- and low-income communities. In Los Angeles one of Teach For America's alumni, Brian Johnson, runs Larchmont Charter Schools, currently a two-campus K–6 (soon to be K–8) network of schools that brings higher-income and lower-income students together and offers a project-based "constructivist" curriculum featuring multi-age classes. In September 2010 Larchmont Schools became the highest-performing charter network in L.A., with both of its schools landing in the top thirty of the more than eight hundred public schools in the district.

A growing number of organizations and philanthropists are determined to accelerate these kinds of innovations through fostering social entrepreneurship in the education arena. New Profit, Inc., a national venture-philanthropy organization, invests in supporting entrepreneurs to expand innovative organizations that will impact the social mobility of low-income Americans. New Profit has provided invaluable funding and many other forms of assistance to Teach For America, KIPP, Achievement First, New Leaders for New Schools, and Stand for Children, among others. The New Schools Venture Fund, Echoing Green, and the Mind Trust each seek to identify such innovations at an earlier stage and provide important seed funding and launch support.

We can imagine many reasons for insufficient innovation in education. Historically, the system felt little pressure to solve the problem of educating low-income children, given our assumptions about the role of socioeconomic factors in school success and given weak accountability systems. Moreover, we have invested precious little in research and development. The progress made along these dimensions in recent years will hopefully gain steam and usher in an entirely new era of innovation, but as ever the key will be cultivating the pioneers. Just as many of the innovators in medicine are doctors who understand the specific nature of the problems they confront, the pioneers in education will be educators who understand the possibility of transformational change and how to effect it. We must encourage their entrepreneurship, stoking their initiatives with start-up investments, fellowships, and other forms of support.

CONCLUSION

To realize a vision of educational excellence and equity, we will need to develop an educational leadership pipeline to propagate transformational schools, the political leadership and advocacy infrastructure to create an environment conducive to their success, and new innovations to increase the efficiency and effectiveness of their efforts. At each turn, success will rely on people who have internalized the lessons of transformational education. And so we come to a central question: How do we find and develop more of these people?

6

TRANSFORMATIONAL TEACHING AS THE FOUNDATION FOR TRANSFORMATIONAL CHANGE

WHEN MY SON BENJAMIN WAS EIGHT, he had to write a school paper. His assignment was to interview someone about a problem she had tackled, and Benjamin decided to interview me about the first year of Teach For America. I guess I had never told him about this, and he was getting excited to hear how it all began. He dutifully took notes. I finished the story and thought we were done. He seemed totally energized by the account. But then he said, "I have one more question."

"I just don't understand," he said, "how if this is such a big problem—you know, kids not having the chance to have a good education—why would you ask people with no experience right out of college to solve it?"

Literally before I could think, I said, "Benjamin . . . ," in what must have sounded like an exasperated voice.

He shot back, "Well, I have to ask because I have to write the paper!"

I had to laugh. I was struck by his question because it reminded me how counterintuitive this effort seems at first blush. Indeed, twenty years into this, it seems that I'm still spending just as much time as I did on day one trying to get people to understand what it is that we're doing. And my eight year old had gone straight to the heart of the matter.

So I sat back down with Benjamin and tried to do my best to answer his question. I started by sharing my view that although it's true that experience can be invaluable, there's also a power in inexperience—that it can make a huge difference to channel the energy of young people, before they know what's "impossible" and when they still have endless energy, against a problem that many have long since given up on. They can set and meet goals that seem impossible to others who know more about how the world works.

I think Benjamin got the idea that sometimes youthful idealism is exactly what we need to tackle our most entrenched social problems. But he declared himself done before I could try to explain how the experience of teaching successfully in our low-income communities is shaping future leaders in ways that will have significant long-term impacts on the injustice of educational inequity.

FOUNDATIONS OF CHANGE IN NEW ORLEANS

Todd Purvis, a principal of one of New Orleans's high-performing schools, joined Teach For America's New Orleans corps in 2003. Assigned to Langston Hughes Elementary in New Orleans, he taught in an overcrowded classroom that had only three walls. The fourth was a wall of bookshelves installed a foot off the ground and going five feet into the air. His smaller second and third graders found they could enter the classroom by sliding on the floor under the bookshelves from the hall. "When anyone came to visit, that was the highlight," he recalled.

The overcrowding in Todd's classroom had reached barely manageable levels because neighborhood schools were in turmoil. Todd's was a "failing" school, but it was just above the corrective action line and so became a school where parents could choose to send children who were attending nearby schools below that line. Even though the actual performance gap between those other schools and his was pretty small, students were pouring into his ill-prepared campus. "There was no space to move," he said.

On one of the first Fridays of Todd's third year of teaching, he used an article from the local newspaper about a coming storm to teach his fifth graders about sequencing and the "main idea." The "main idea" of the article was that the hurricane was projected to loop back on itself and head to Florida. Todd went about his weekend, prepping for the next week of school, when he received an alarming message from a close friend and fellow Teach For America alumnus. "Do we need to get out of here?" his friend asked. Only then did Todd learn that Katrina was coming and that Mayor Ray Nagin was telling everyone to get out of the city as quickly as they could. Todd and a couple of teacher friends evacuated to a friend's family home in tiny Manny, Louisiana.

Todd recalls the next few days as a blur of shock and sadness. His phone didn't work, and all he could do was watch the television in horror all day. "I saw one of my students—a fifth grader—walking through the water on television. She was carrying two kids—two of her sisters—and the water was up to her midthigh. It was horrible, but I was so glad to know she was alive." After four or five days, with only two T-shirts and a pair of shorts, and the realization that he could not return to New Orleans, Todd drove north with a plan that he would stay with some friends and his parents until he could go back.

Meanwhile, my colleagues and I across the country were glued to the television as well. As our New Orleans staff members scrambled to try to track down our corps members (all of whom were eventually accounted for), we watched the news, terribly saddened as the deficiencies of our public infrastructure drove tens of thousands of families out of their city. Like most of the country, the Teach For America community was searching for ways to help.

I checked in with Mike Feinberg, the KIPP cofounder who runs the KIPP schools in Houston. The children our New Orleans corps members had been teaching were displaced all across the state of Louisiana and beyond; many had been uprooted by bus to Houston, ending up in the Astrodome, among other places. We at Teach For America were trying to decide how to redeploy our New Orleans corps members when Mike came up with an idea. He had access to a vacant school in Houston for one year, and a team that had been preparing to open a KIPP school in New Orleans had also been displaced. Mike said he would provide the administration and the building if we wanted to rally our displaced corps members to recruit students and be their teachers.

Within just a couple of days, Todd and his fellow corps members, now scattered across the country, were getting phone calls from Teach For America staff members explaining that a group of teachers was heading to Houston to start a school for New Orleans kids who were, at the time, sleeping in and outside of the Houston Astrodome. "Do you guys want to be part of this?" the staff member asked. Todd and his friends instantly signed on. Todd was sure some of his kids from Langston Hughes were in the Astrodome, and he could not stand feeling so helpless. The school was to open immediately, so Todd and his friends jumped in the car and drove twenty straight hours to Houston. Todd moved onto the couch of a family who agreed to host some teachers. "Luckily, they had this college-aged son, and I borrowed some clothes," he explained.

The next day, Todd, along with twenty-seven other Teach For America corps members and eight alumni, walked up and down the aisles of the Astrodome signing up kids to attend their new school, "New Orleans West." In a mere ten days, NOW College Prep— under the leadership of Gary Robichaux, who was the soon-to-be principal of the KIPP school that had been planned for New Orleans—was born.

From its inception, NOW College Prep was a school that served children facing inconceivable challenges. These 400 kindergarten through eighth graders had been ripped away from everything they knew. They were largely homeless, and subsequent studies showed that many were suffering from post-traumatic stress disorder. Yet Gary and Todd and their colleagues decided that they would not let external circumstances, as horrific as they were, undermine the potential of these children. So they designed and delivered an educational experience in record time—one that came to fulfill its promise.

Despite the disruption to their lives, the average NOW College Prep student improved 15 percentile points in reading and 27 percentile points in math according to the Stanford 10 test in their first year in the school. In Todd's classroom 85 percent passed the Texas assessments, more than double the pass rates for other displaced New Orleans children across Houston and comparing favorably with many students in Houston who had not just gone through the trauma of Katrina.

Todd's experience leading children to academic success changed his perspective, and the course of his life. Reminiscing about his teaching days, Todd described the transformative experience that so many of our teachers have when they see the potential their students have to excel academically:

Going through that year in Houston is really the reason I'm still here in a school. I remember my last year at Langston Hughes [before the storm]—things weren't changing. The whole system was absolutely broken. . . . Our principal was very hardworking and dedicated, and we had a pretty decent staff, but still nothing was changing. NOW rejuvenated my sense of possibility and really reset my expectations of students. . . . We were challenged every day but working with incredible kids, and we were all so bonded out of Katrina. What happened was horrible and undeserved, but what came out of it and the possibility that a lot of us felt are, I think, why so many of us are still with it.

I met Todd at the New Orleans school where he is now a principal, Central City Academy, a KIPP school. Like many KIPP schools, Todd's campus has more students and families signing on than spaces available. Students are chosen for acceptance by a random lottery to ensure fairness. In 2007 the school opened with 90 fifth graders, 8 percent of whom were on level in reading, 8 percent in math. Students brought with them the range of challenges facing children in the poorest neighborhoods in New Orleans, and many had special needs. According to nationally referenced assessments, 80 percent of Central City's incoming students were in the lowest quartile in reading and math.

Today, Central City Academy serves 360 children in grades five through eight. As of seventh grade, students have progressed so far that they are three-quarters of a year *above* grade level based on national assessments, with another year of middle school at Central City Academy still ahead. Todd has closed the achievement gap for his students and put them on track to go to college. "Even in the face of tremendous challenges, I know our kids will successfully climb the mountain through college," he told me. "Success is about how hard you work, not where you are from. Our kids work incredibly hard every day so that they will be successful in college."

Todd's story—that of a talented new teacher whose experience leading students through enormous challenges to dramatic achievement galvanized a lifelong dedication to solving educational inequity and gave him the foundational experiences necessary for success—is precisely the experience we hope all of our corps members will share. It is the story of the transformative power of a successful teaching experience, one that serves as a foundation for a lifetime of leadership and advocacy for children.

PERSONAL TRANSFORMATION
THROUGH TRANSFORMATIONAL TEACHING

Although Katrina makes for a particularly dramatic variation, Todd's story is representative of the stories of most of the classroom, school, district, policy, and political leaders described in this book and of Teach For America's theory of change about how to eliminate educational inequity. Highly effective teachers in low-income communities change kids' lives—*and kids change theirs.*

Maurice Thomas, the teacher introduced in Chapter 1 who led all of his students to be accepted to college, told me that his experience in the classroom completely changed his life. "The students, parents, and educators I have met will always be with me," he said. "Without this experience I would probably be in my last year of law school, but now I cannot imagine myself working in any other field. I intend to eventually go back to school to receive an advanced degree in educational leadership and open my own school. I feel like teaching has unleashed my full potential, and if need be, to ensure we solve this problem, I intend to be the first Teach For America governor, in the great state of Wisconsin."

We did a very informal survey of many of the Teach For America corps members and alumni introduced in this book. Virtually all of them said that they were confident that if they had not joined Teach For America, they would not be pushing the frontier of education reform today. Tim Daly said that instead of working at The New Teacher Project, he would likely have pursued a Ph.D. in history. Sehba Ali, instead of founding and running successful schools, would have been a psychologist. Michelle Rhee, instead of pioneering education reforms, thinks she would probably have been a lawyer, as do Mike Feinberg and Reid Whitaker.

The transformative experience of leading children in low-income communities to great progress plays out across our corps and alumni force. While Teach For America asks for a two-year commitment from its recruits (the vast majority of whom were not education majors and not, they tell us, headed into education), more than 60 percent of our 20,000-plus alumni are working in education, with about half of those still in the classroom. Those working in education from outside the classroom are mostly working in schools or districts, or in organizations meant to support them. Of those alumni who *leave* education, going into a vast array of careers from law to medicine, from government to journalism to business, more than 60 percent have jobs that relate in some way to schools or low-income communities—for example, as doctors practicing in public health or policy advisers working on education issues.

Many of the new models of excellence on the front lines of the fight against educational inequity were founded or are being driven by current or former teachers whose conviction, determination, and leadership were developed in the classroom. Today, virtually all KIPP school leaders proved their mettle and built their skills by putting children on a new academic path in their classrooms—and nearly two-thirds of the network's principals started their careers as Teach For America corps members. (A little fewer than one-third of the network's current teachers are Teach For America corps members or alumni.) Similar stories play out at YES Prep, Achievement First, Uncommon Schools, and many of the most successful traditional district schools in the country. The path to transformational leadership is through the transformative experience of seeing and fulfilling the promise of children in low-income communities.

I think the reasons for this phenomenon are complex but clear. First, teachers who have taught successfully develop an unshakable conviction about what is possible through education for children growing up in economically disadvantaged circumstances. Their personal knowledge of the potential of their students and of teachers and schools, and their love for their students, drives a deep and personal motivation to right the injustice of educational disadvantage. This understanding becomes the root of their career choices and professional decisions and the driving force behind their bold goals, perseverance in pursuit of them, and persuasiveness with others.

Second, these teachers understand what it takes to put children in low-income communities on a level playing field. They reject any particular silver-bullet theory because they know—they have experienced firsthand—that there is no "one" thing that will solve this problem. They appreciate the extent of the challenges facing their students and know just how much it takes to provide them with the supports and experiences to reach those expectations.

Third, because teaching successfully is itself an act of leadership, these teachers gain the confidence and mindsets critical to effecting change on a larger scale. Washington D.C.'s Kaya Henderson summed up this effect beautifully: "I think people in this field have gotten so beaten down by not being able to accomplish big things that they don't have a sense of possibility anymore," she said, adding, "If I never learned anything else from Teach For America, I learned to have a sense of possibility. Other people say you can't— actually you can, and you just do."

It is striking that the very same themes of action that distinguish our highly effective teachers distinguish highly effective school leaders, system leaders, policy makers, and all education reformers who are making a real impact. Just as in the classroom, success is a function of the hard work of great leadership—pursuing a vision of change, investing others in working hard to reach it, working deliberately and strategically, accessing whatever resources are necessary to ensure that education is changing children's lives, and continuously improving.

FOUNDATIONS OF CHANGE IN LOS ANGELES

Back in Teach For America's first year, in 1990, we started placing about two hundred corps members a year in Los Angeles. In 1991 one of these corps members was Ana Ponce. Originally from Mexico, Ana had grown up in the Pico Union area of Los Angeles, one of the lowest-income neighborhoods in the city and an area with dismal high school graduation rates. Driven by her personal experience of witnessing the academic failure of her peers, Ana initially committed just two years to Teach For America because she was drawn to the idea of service. She says that when she saw the reality facing her students and their unfulfilled potential, she realized she had to make a longer commitment. So, after leading her bilingual kindergarten students to impressive academic gains, Ana attended Columbia Teachers College in New York and earned her master's degree in bilingual-bicultural education. She then returned to Los Angeles.

Ana became a founding teacher at the Accelerated School, a South Central L.A. charter school opened in 1994 in a leased church social hall in the historical shadow of the 1992 Los Angeles riots. About half of the neighborhood's residents had never made it to tenth grade, and almost half of the households earned less than $15,000 a year. Ana and the other teachers brought what they called a "relentless pursuit of excellence" to the school, proving through their hard work and student performance that demographics do not determine academic outcomes. Based on its phenomenal student progress, *Time* named the school its "Elementary School of the Year" in 2001. The Accelerated School outperformed other public schools in the area several times over on standardized tests, as students' Stanford Achievement Test scores jumped 93 percent in just a few years.[1]

Inspired by her students' dramatic progress in response to the school's philosophy of introducing lagging learners to the same challenges as gifted students, and by the school's commitment to working closely with the community and parents, Ana looked for ways to spread those approaches to students in the neighborhood where she had grown up. She became the principal and then executive director of another start-up charter school, Camino Nuevo Charter Academy, as part of a larger community-development effort initiated by community leader Philip Lance. Ana worked with other educators, about a third of whom were Teach For America alumni, to build a network of schools that have helped change her community's vision of what is possible for, and what to expect from, children living in low-income neighborhoods. Camino Nuevo now operates four campuses and has plans to expand to a fifth site. All of the network's schools are rated highly on the state's Academic Performance Index (API), a formula that looks at student achievement and doesn't build in extra credit for serving children living in poverty.

Teach For America alumni are embedded throughout this high-performing network's leadership. At last count, two principals, four assistant principals, three central office administrators, and one school's director of bilingual education all got their start in education through Teach For America. Under the leadership of alumna Heather McManus, one of the network's schools, Camino Nuevo High School, was recognized by the state as one of the top-twenty high schools in Los Angeles. Under the leadership of alumnae Kate Sobel and Heather McManus, the K–8 campus became a California Distinguished School in 2010.

The success story of Ana, Heather, Kate, and Camino Nuevo has become more and more representative in the rapidly changing education landscape in Los Angeles. In that city and many others, Teach For America's teachers and alumni are working alongside many others to lead classrooms and schools that are changing the prospects for kids. At last count, there were forty-two Teach For America alumni heading schools in the Los Angeles region—and many of those schools are among the region's highest performing. Today, not just Camino Nuevo but several of the top-twenty highest-performing high schools in Los Angeles are run by Teach For America alumni, and all of those schools have at least 80 percent of the students qualifying for free and reduced lunch.

Donna Foote, a former *Newsweek* correspondent, spent the 2005–2006 school year following Teach For America corps members in what must have been one of the country's most challenging settings—Locke High School in South Los Angeles. For years, Locke High School had been a tragic example of failure. Donna found that Locke had a freshman class of about 1,000 students in 2001. Four years later only 240 students graduated, and only 30 of those had earned the credits necessary to even apply to a California state college.[2] Donna published a compelling account of several teachers' experience in *Relentless Pursuit: A Year in the Trenches with Teach For America*. The book ends after a year, but looking back now, it provides a firsthand account of the formation of a leadership force for change.

The first third of the book provides plenty of fodder for skeptics who might wonder what Teach For America is thinking in placing naive and inexperienced teachers in the nation's most challenging schools. Donna brings into stark relief corps members' daily encounters and reactions to violence and poverty, as well as their struggles and failures in the classroom. As the reader progresses, however, Donna reveals the students' and teachers' perseverance, grit, resilience, and growth. In fact, we see over the course of her book the beginning of the transformation of new struggling teachers into uncompromising and determined leaders. Still, few readers would have envisioned that the teachers they met in Chapter 1 would be fighting for educational equity today.

In the book we are introduced to Rachelle Snyder as the "stereotypical southern California girl" who had a "carefree" and relatively privileged upbringing in the Mission Hills section of San Diego. We watch as she struggles to address the challenges of poverty in her special education students' lives but also leads them to succeed in ways they did not believe they could. The next year Rachelle had an even greater impact and was recognized by the mayor for her teaching. She stayed on at Locke for one year beyond her two-year commitment and then went to work at a nonprofit. Just recently, she left that nonprofit to return to teach at one of the schools created when Locke was broken up under new leadership.

Hrag Hamalian, the introspective former high school wrestler whom we meet as a promising but somewhat uncertain, aimless, fun-loving college senior, and who at first struggled mightily to get control in his fifth-period biology class of boys, became the de facto leader of the Biology Department at Locke, rewrote the curriculum, and worked his second year training other teachers. Deciding he wanted to make an even bigger impact, Hrag applied and was accepted to an organization called Building Excellent Schools that trains urban school leaders. He has now founded a new school called Valor Academy that serves primarily Latino low-income children and is staffed entirely by Teach For America corps member and alumni. The school just completed its first year, and the results are truly inspiring. According to the rigorous and nationally normed Stanford 10 assessments, the school's first cohort of fifth grade students moved from the 20th to the 51st percentile in just one year. Put differently, the fifth grade class started the school year at a mid–third grade level and ended up on grade level, achieving two and a half years' worth of academic growth during that time.

The book also follows Taylor Rifkin, who grew up in a family of educators but was at first drawn to Teach For America, according to Donna Foote, because her family was well off and she could afford to be a "low-paid humanitarian." Taylor, we learn, figured "she would join TFA for two years, with luck do some good, and worry about what to do with the rest of her life later." But over the course of the book, we see the influence of transformative teaching on both the teacher and the students, as her gang-involved students became immersed in *Romeo and Juliet* on the way to posting an average of 2.9 years' worth of literacy growth. After her two-year commitment Taylor moved over to teach at Ànimo Watts II Charter High School, one of the schools that would soon play into the reorganization of Locke itself. Today, she is dean at the high-performing Achievement First Bushwick middle school in Brooklyn.

In the book we also meet Phillip Gedeon, a hardworking (but struggling B-student) college student activist whose mother was "devastated" to learn he was joining Teach For America. Phillip was inspired to join, in part, by his own experience growing up in America as a black child of a single mother and his belief that that experience could make him a strong teacher. We see Phillip's constantly evolving instructional methods (including an intense geometry boot camp) lead his students to solid mastery of difficult geometry concepts at Locke, and we see Phillip's growing conviction that teaching and education are his calling. Phillip has since become a math teaching coach for LAUSD (Los Angeles United School District) as he earns his Ph.D. in urban school leadership.

Chad Soleo, the 2001 corps member profiled in *Relentless Pursuit* who once viewed Teach For America as a detour on the way to law school and worked hard during the course of the book to stem the chaos and support the new teachers as an assistant principal at Locke, today works for the Green Dot charter and turnaround organization to manage the cluster of schools that has replaced Locke High School. In just a couple of years since the school was converted, there has been a 36 percent increase in student enrollment, and 95 percent of the students have stayed in school (whereas in years past more than two-thirds of students dropped out). More students are passing the state assessments — 10 percent more in both math and language arts.[3] Everyone involved is wary of any celebrations yet, as the schools created from the old Locke High School have a long way to go. But they are moving quickly in the right direction.

Teach For America's executive director in Los Angeles, Paul Miller, thinks about the changing landscape in terms of the city's turbulent history of racial and socioeconomic tensions. He told me about the experience of flipping through old "redlining" maps at a local university — maps from the 1940s and '50s that told businesses like banks and insurers where "slums" existed and mortgages, loans, and insurance policies should not be provided. Paul was struck by the near-perfect alignment between those historical maps' boundaries and the frontiers of the achievement gap that still mark the city. But today, Paul takes anyone who is willing through a virtual tour of Los Angeles's difficult history juxtaposed with the beacons of dramatic success in those same places. Ana Ponce's pace-setting Camino Nuevo High School is, Paul points out, in the same MacArthur Park area that has historically been infamous for drug dealers and gang shoot-outs.

Watts — the site of both the 1960s riots and the 1992 riots in the wake of the Rodney King beating — is another area where it is striking to contrast historical turbulence and school failure with recent changes. In the past decade the average API (Academic Performance Index) growth in Watts was 195 points, the equivalent of almost halving the gap between schools in Watts and schools in Beverly Hills during roughly the same period.[4] "I was at a charter school recently in Watts, and the principal showed me a beam in the school that is charred from the Watts riots in 1965," Paul told me. "This school is, today, loaded with Teach For America teachers and outperforming every school in the area." He continued, "We now have these proof points all over the city, right in the most intensively hit and underserved areas—and they are turning the history of despair in these communities into a story of hope."

There are many reasons for the progress in Los Angeles—and they go well beyond Teach For America's influence. But if we removed the growing force of successful teachers Teach For America has placed in Los Angeles over the past twenty years, we would take away a vital part of the force for change.

FOUNDATIONS OF CHANGE
IN CITIES ACROSS THE COUNTRY

In communities across the country, the force of Teach For America alumni is growing toward a point of critical mass, and in all of these places, we see tangible manifestations of our theory of change. Teach For America's work to build an enduring movement to realize educational equity in America is gaining traction as our earliest cohorts of corps members assume positions of influence.

I remember the warm reception we received from Houston's civic leaders when we began placing corps members there in 1991. Houston is an entrepreneurial city, and many there seemed to love the initiative and spunk that Teach For America represented. They loved the notion of young, idealistic teachers in Houston Independent School District classrooms. But I remember discussions with business leaders who made it clear that they were under no illusion that Teach For America would "change the system." "*Nothing* can change HISD," they warned.

Twenty years later, the charter school networks started by Chris Barbic and Mike Feinberg are serving more than 10,000 students and in the midst of growth plans that have them serving 15 percent of HISD's student population in the next decade. And today, HISD is led by a superintendent who has vowed to bring the learning from these networks inside his system. He has hired Teach For America alumnus Jeremy Beard, formerly the principal of an extremely successful charter school in the Rio Grande Valley, to lead this initiative. Jeremy partners with Ann Best, our former executive director in Houston and another Teach For America alumna who serves as HISD's chief talent officer, to reshape the administration and teaching staffs of nine schools designated for "turnaround." Harvard economist Roland Fryer has masterminded this initiative, with the goal of bringing what he has seen work through his educational research—a focus on "human capital," more time, high-dosage tutoring, and rigorous culture and expectations—into one demonstration project. Today, Houston's civic leadership has an entirely different understanding of what is possible for schools to accomplish and of the possibility of significant change.

I remember our early days in Baltimore, too. We had started placing teachers there in 1991, when Bob Embry, a philanthropic force in the city, wrote me a short letter pledging to do whatever it took to bring Teach For America into the system.

For years, I viewed Baltimore City Public Schools as one of the most entrenched of our district partners. In 2005, of the school districts serving the nation's fifty-largest cities, Baltimore was ranked forty-sixth out of fifty, with a graduation rate of 41.5 percent.[5]

Twenty years after we first placed teachers in Baltimore, I am amazed to see the winds of change that are effecting measurable progress for the children in that city. The system's brilliant CEO, Andres Alonso, arrived in Baltimore after serving as Joel Klein's deputy chancellor in New York. In describing his experience to Teach For America's board of directors, Alonso said he was surprised to arrive in Baltimore and realize that the ground troops were ready and waiting, in the form of hundreds of Teach For America alumni. They were running the local efforts of New Leaders for New Schools, which has already recruited a quarter of the system's principals. Others were managing the KIPP Network's growing presence in Baltimore and leading the New Teacher Project's effort to train principals in Baltimore in selecting new teachers. Today, thirteen alumni work as principals, and twenty-five hold key roles in the central district.

Today, among districts serving high populations of low-income students, Baltimore is showing some success. On NAEP assessments, the district's low-income African American students outperformed the same demographic in Chicago, Cleveland, Detroit, D.C., Los Angeles, and Philadelphia, among others. The school system's dropout rate fell by a third over three years, and the incidences of parents withdrawing students from the system have been cut in half. Student suspensions have dropped by almost 40 percent since 2007, and the enrollment has increased for two consecutive years after four decades of decline. Of course, as Andres is the first to say, much remains to be done. He has placed the growth of Teach For America at the center of his agenda, given the role he believes it plays in catalyzing fundamental change.

On the other side of the country, since 1991 Teach For America has also been placing corps members in Oakland, California. At that time, there was very little momentum for change in Oakland's district, which was historically one of California's lowest performing.

Today, it is one of the fastest-improving districts in the state, with one of the most significant changes being the proliferation of a new set of schools through a district effort initiated in part and later run by Teach For America alumna Hae-sin Thomas, who began teaching in Oakland in 1993. Today, more than 10 percent of Oakland's schools are led by Teach For America alumni, including some recognized as among the highest performing and fastest improving. An alum-led effort called the Oakland Teaching Fellows provides, together with Teach For America, two-thirds of the district's new-teacher hires. And a group of alumni led by Hae-sin and Jonathan Klein, who is also the chief program officer of one of the largest education foundations in the community, has formed Great Oakland Public Schools to engage the leadership of Oakland's school district in finding innovative ways to achieve fiscal responsibility while sustaining and advancing effective reforms; this group has been instrumental in pushing for and winning recent changes.

From the East Coast in New York City, Newark, Philadelphia, Baltimore, and Washington, D.C., to the Southeast in New Orleans and Houston, to the Midwest in Chicago, to the Southwest in Phoenix, to the West Coast in Los Angeles and the Bay Area, to many communities in between, Teach For America corps members and alumni are fueling many efforts to change the prospects for our nation's urban children.

FOUNDATIONS OF CHANGE IN RURAL AMERICA

Talk of the achievement gap often conjures up images of children in blighted urban neighborhoods, yet children in rural areas often face similarly bleak educational opportunities. Elisa Villanueva Beard, Teach For America's chief operating officer, told me about growing up in the Rio Grande Valley along the Texas-Mexico border and experiencing low expectations in the form of a silent assumption that students in the valley do not go to college. "I was a top student, president of the Student Council, and involved in everything," she said. "And rarely did anyone at school talk to me about college. And if they did, the expectation was that I would go to the local college and not consider exploring the opportunities beyond my comfort zone."

Elisa ended up going to DePauw University in Indiana before joining Teach For America as a corps member in Phoenix. She later returned home to the valley and served as Teach For America's executive director in the region. Elisa has a deep love for her community, an acute concern about the low expectations it holds for its children, and a real hope for its future. "The Rio Grande Valley is filled with talented, diverse, and unique individuals," she told me, "but we are too often plagued with a culture of low expectations for what is possible for every child to achieve in our poverty-stricken community. It is a tragedy that our kids are not expected to achieve at the same levels as their more affluent peers across the state and country, that we don't teach or foster a sense of hope for students to dream big, that most students do not deeply believe they are in full control of their life prospects." Elisa shared her reflections on the roots of this issue and on how to change it:

> Things here have always been the way they have been; most of our teachers are products of the public schools of the valley, go to the local university that does not demand excellence of them either, and then are funneled back into the education system. That is what they know, and all along nobody understands that it is a massive perpetuating cycle of low expectations for all. The people of the region are eager for something better when they realize that it can be better.

The more and more our communities are able to experience what having an excellent education can do to a child, a family, and then a community, the impact of that will be unstoppable because the great and smart people in our region will demand and provide more of it.

Illustrating Elisa's concerns, across the region where Teach For America works in the valley, there are still roughly 5,000 students a year who should be graduating but are neither graduating nor getting their "graduation equivalency diploma." Perhaps a third of those who do graduate are labeled "college ready" by the state, yet the "gatekeeper" courses at local colleges find that about 50 percent of them are not actually ready to perform at the college level. (And those numbers do not even include students who decide on their own that they are not ready and so enroll in local colleges' remedial courses.)

Robert Carreon, Teach For America's executive director in the Rio Grande Valley, was himself born and raised in a small border community and requested an assignment to teach in the Rio Grande Valley as a corps member. Like Elisa, he sees both frustration and promise in the valley: "Not too long ago," he told me, "we were looking for data on student performance for the valley from 1990 and 1991. The state Web site was just blank for the valley. Everywhere else had data, but we didn't. It was like we didn't exist," he said. "But now, people are watching what's happening here. We have come a very long way. In the past five years, we have seen increases in performance on all the measures that matter—high school completion, proficiency on assessments, and numbers of students graduating college-ready."

One of the education initiatives that people are watching in the Rio Grande Valley is the IDEA Public School network. (IDEA stands for Individuals Dedicated to Excellence and Achievement.)

An open-enrollment public charter network founded by two Teach For America alumni, JoAnn Gama and Tom Torkelson, the IDEA schools serve 7,000 children across the valley, many of whom are growing up in *colonias* that lack basic infrastructure like water, electricity, and drainage. Many IDEA students and their families are migrant workers, picking crops across the country at harvest time.

Tom got the idea for IDEA in his second year of teaching, when he realized that the only way to radically reset the educational experience for his fourth grade students, many of whom were three or four grade levels behind, was to create a distinct "school within a school"—an educational setting with its own culture, curriculum, and schedule. The following year Tom, along with JoAnn Gama and Hannah Famiglietti, launched IDEA Academy, with 75 students, within the structure of their school. By any objective measure, their students were wildly successful. Student academic achievement increased significantly. But the district closed down the aging campus where the program was housed, and their entire student population was scattered throughout the system as part of a redistricting effort. After restarting the program at a new school, Tom decided he needed to run his own school to fully realize his vision; in January 2001 Tom wrote an application envisioning the IDEA charter school and submitted it to the State of Texas.

Ten years later IDEA operates sixteen schools, starting up two to four new schools a year. IDEA's 7,000 students are now outperforming many students in high-income schools across the state. The network's flagship high school, which incorporates an international baccalaureate curriculum, was recently ranked the top-performing high school in the Rio Grande Valley and the *thirteenth-best high school* in the entire United States by *U.S. News and World Report*. (Until recently, this school was run by Jeremy Beard, who is now managing HISD's turnaround effort described earlier in this chapter.) Every single school in the network, and just recently the entire network itself, won an "exemplary" rating from the state—an honor achieved by only 72 of the 1,200 districts in the state (and IDEA was the largest serving a majority of low-income students). When you ask Tom about that success, he turns the focus back on the students. "What our students have achieved is remarkable," he says.

Robert Carreon, our executive director in the region, lists other strong signs of promise involving our growing alumni community. Scott Therkelsen (who has a master's degree in mechanical engineering from MIT) taught ninth grade science and math in Donna, Texas, for three years before assuming the role of dean of instruction at his school in 2008. Today, he is responsible for interviewing and hiring new teachers and overseeing professional development for all the teachers in his school based on instructional areas of need. Just down the highway, Leonore Tyler, who has been teaching or leading a school in the Rio Grande Valley since arriving there as a Teach For America corps member in 1993, is the founding principal of the Career, College, and Technology Academy, which supports students who have not graduated from high school due to failed classes or exit examinations. Since the school's founding in the fall of 2007, hundreds of students have graduated who would not have otherwise.

Teach For America also now has a number of teachers in its corps who grew up in the valley and were pushed and inspired to attend college by their Teach For America teachers. Last year, four new corps members at one valley high school had all been taught by the same Teach For America Advanced Placement Physics teacher five years before. One of those students, Marco Martinez, recently testified to the impact his teacher had made. "Now that I look back, I was probably one of the more uncooperative students she had," Marco admits. "But in the long run, her *relentlessness*—to use TFA slang—did me well. Ms. Sung never gave up on me. Ever."

Within the group of rural communities that Teach For America serves, the Rio Grande Valley is no anomaly. Our teachers and alumni are making a real difference in other rural areas as well. Since 1991, when we began our work in the network of communities in Mississippi and Arkansas known as the Mississippi Delta, we have brought almost 1,500 new teachers to the region. Today, we have more than 500 corps members in the midst of their two-year commitments and more than 150 alumni all across the greater Delta region.

As in other communities, a number of alumni in the Delta have gravitated to school leadership. Ten Teach For America alumni are now school leaders, principals, or instructional leaders in Delta schools. In one small district, the elementary, middle, and high schools are each headed by Teach For America alumni.

Scott Shirey, who joined Teach For America in 1998, founded the KIPP Delta Public Schools, a network of four KIPP schools based in the small eastern Arkansas towns of Helena and Blytheville. All four of the KIPP schools are led by Teach For America Delta alumni, and more than 70 percent of their schools' staffs are either first- or second-year corps members or alumni. When KIPP Delta expands and opens three additional high schools, its leaders project that they will be producing more college-ready seniors than all the other high schools in the eight eastern Arkansas counties around them.

The list of ways that our alumni are catalyzing change in the Delta extends from small but important projects on individual school campuses to large-scale interventions across the state. The Sunflower County Freedom Project was at first a summer program to provide academic enrichment, started by three alumni while they pursued advanced degrees. Today, it has grown into a year-round program offering extracurricular activities, community service, leadership development, and educational trips to prepare students to enroll and excel in four-year colleges or universities. More than 300 students have participated in its programs since 1999. Another team of alumni, convinced that they could influence students' academic achievement through effecting policy change, earned their public policy degrees and formed Mississippi First. Their nonprofit advocacy organization informs and steers legislation and policies related to education, such as economic development, health care, tolerance, and civic participation.

FUELING AN UNSTOPPABLE MOVEMENT

Teach For America is working to expand the pipeline of transformational leadership until that tipping point moment when the movement to eliminate educational inequity becomes unstoppable. We are determined to build on the foundation of our first twenty years to play our part in reaching the point at which the achievement gap finally begins to close on an aggregate level. This means we must become still larger and more diverse, developing a critical mass of leaders, even more of whom share the racial or economic background, or both, of our schools and communities. It means partnering with more communities around the country. It has taken twenty years to develop an alumni force 20,000 strong, and we are working to double this number in the next five years and to grow it exponentially in the next twenty.

Fulfilling Teach For America's potential also means ensuring that our corps members are, more consistently, transformational teachers—that they are changing the trajectories of their students and in the process gaining the foundational experience necessary for effective long-term educational leadership and advocacy. Achieving this goal means we need to continue developing our understanding of what differentiates the most successful teachers and strengthening our pre-service and ongoing efforts to develop corps members.

Finally, while we work to increase the scale and diversity of our corps and to ensure our teachers' greater success, we are also focused on accelerating their leadership in areas that we know are most pressing and critical to the broader reform effort, with a focus on redoubling our efforts to support alumni who pursue careers in teaching and school and district leadership; increasing the number of alumni who win elective office, serve as key policy advisers, and lead advocacy initiatives; and providing alumni with the space and support to develop game-changing innovations.

CONCLUSION

Although I don't think my son Benjamin could have understood the long-term power of Teach For America when he was eight, I am hopeful that as he grows up he will see the evidence all around him. This year Teach For America will bring in more new corps members than we did over the course of our entire first decade. When reflecting on the fact that the alumni produced in that first decade are now at the center of many of the promising efforts to expand educational opportunity, it's inspiring to envision the impact of an exponentially larger group. This year's corps members will be better trained to succeed with their students than ever before—and better supported to maximize their impact as alumni. And, as Teach For America works to get bigger and better, this is only the beginning. Given the personal transformation that occurs when teachers succeed with their students, I have no doubt that the growing network of Teach For America corps members and alumni will develop into a powerful force for fundamental change. Because they started early in their careers, they will have a chance to make a significant impact on the problem of educational inequity, as complex and massive as it is. Ultimately, in part because of their efforts, I am convinced our education system will improve on a national level.

CONCLUSION
WHETHER WE WILL

W HAT IS SO POWERFULLY MOTIVATING for the growing force of Teach For America alumni is the jarring discrepancy between their students' typical performance and the potential they have for dramatic academic achievement.

Steven Farr, who helped me write this book, thinks a lot about his former student Juan Orozco. Juan was one of the many migrant students Steven taught as a 1993 corps member on the Texas-Mexico border. Juan, like many of his classmates, spent summers—and often parts of the school year—working in the fields harvesting vegetables and fruit. Like many of Steven's students, Juan lived in one of the area's *colonias*.

Steven taught Juan as both a sophomore and a junior. Like his classmates, Juan was bright and capable but far behind where he needed to be to get on track to college. For many of Steven's students, passing the state's assessment of the most rudimentary literacy skills—a requirement for graduation—was a real challenge, and Steven fought to keep some of his students who had failed the exam as sophomores from dropping out.

Steven rallied his students to work hard not only to pass those basic assessments but also to get on track to college. He convinced his principal to let him teach an SAT/ACT preparation course, and his students signed up in droves. Steven worked long hours to improve students' writing, vocabularies, and critical thinking skills. He took busloads of students to Austin for overnight trips to the University of Texas (a "wonderfully harrowing experience," he told me).

In Steven's class, Juan was working hard and making tremendous progress. By every measure, including the basic literacy skills assessments, the writing rubrics Steven used to evaluate essays, and Juan's confidence and leadership among his classmates, Juan was excelling. In the spring, as another season of migrant work approached, Steven and one of his fellow corps members, Stephen Ready, began thinking about ways to ensure that Juan's progress continued. "We sat down with Juan's parents at Pizza Hut and talked about how important it was that Juan keep working on his academics, that we try to identify ways to build his academic skills over the summer," Steven recalls. "It was a tough and delicate conversation, because we were asking Juan's family to make a real financial sacrifice by not having Juan work all season." Juan's parents, immigrants who had come to the United States for the sake of their three children, agreed to make it work. They were eager to do whatever they could to ensure Juan succeeded. (In fact, Steven did not learn until I was gathering information for this story that Juan's mother—who usually didn't work in the summers—took a job at a chicken processing plant while his father was working in the fields to compensate for Juan's absence.)

With Juan's parents' blessing, Steven and his colleagues, and Juan, began investigating academic summer camps and experiences.

They advised Juan on applications and wrote letters of recommendation. Some weeks later Steven asked Juan how the process was going. Juan told him about a couple of summer-camp experiences at local colleges that seemed pretty promising and that he would probably choose. As an aside, he then said, "Oh, and I also got into this program at Oxford, but I only got a partial scholarship. I can't do it, but it looked pretty cool." It turns out Juan had been accepted to a gifted and talented program at Oxford University in England to study Greek and Roman history and archaeology. The cost, including plane fare, was going to be $6,000 or so, and the program had offered him only $3,000. He was moving on to other options.

Steven and Stephen starting spreading the word among teachers and administrators. Just one week later, Juan's classmates and teachers were walking door-to-door selling raffle tickets for the television and other prizes that teachers had donated to the cause. The football coach, the principal, the drama club—all contributed small amounts of money, and the community rallied around this opportunity for Juan. Steven and Stephen gathered money from their friends and contacts. There was even a story in the local newspaper that brought in a few small checks.

At the beginning of the summer, Juan—loaded down with borrowed suitcases and a borrowed camera—said good-bye to his parents. Steven and Stephen drove him the six hours to Houston (to save money on the airfare from the valley), and Juan got on an airplane for the first time in his life—to England.

It's impossible to say with precision the degree of influence that Steven and Stephen had on Juan's success, but there's no doubt that with their help, Juan's educational experience proved transformational. Juan says he had many caring teachers, but that these two teachers had a unique impact. "They brought these big ideas," he told me. Juan also pointed out the difference their encouragement made, especially when he was feeling overwhelmed. When he felt intimidated in the classes at Oxford and shared with Steven how unprepared he felt, Juan recalled, Steven told him "to work through it, stay focused, do the best I could, and that at some point in my college career I would catch up . . . and that I was prepared in other ways that would come in handy to contribute to class discussions." Juan continued:

> I remember later finding out that was true . . . I could relate to these authors—when Adam Smith was talking about factory work, or when we were reading *The Jungle* by Sinclair—more than my other classmates. I remember this conversation when I was sitting in my political theory class discussing *The Wealth of Nations* and everyone was focusing on the virtues of self-interest, the invisible hand, and deregulation and how that is best for capitalism, and I was thinking, "Wait a minute. Smith is about railing against monopolies, international corporate power, and about how there is a lack of economic investment at the local, grassroots level that is not empowering local communities to become economic players."

Listening to Juan's reflections, I understood as Juan himself had that Steven had been right. Juan's challenging background had given him an important perspective, and an excellent education ultimately enabled him to bring it to bear, in his college classes and ultimately in his post-collegiate efforts to strengthen our nation. Today, motivated by his experiences, Juan works at the Sargent Shriver National Center on Poverty Law in Chicago.

Before, during, and after Steven's high school classes, Juan, like millions of other children, was grappling with the challenges of poverty. Like millions of other children, his statistically predicted trajectory was to drop out of high school, perhaps earn a GED, or *maybe* graduate from high school; according to the numbers, college was highly unlikely. Juan beat those odds. In our wealthy nation, there are millions of students with Juan's potential whose promise goes unfulfilled. It should not be this way, and it does not have to be this way.

○ ○ ○

MEGAN BROUSSEAU AND Maurice Thomas, Julie Jackson and Joe Negron, Paul Pastorek and Cami Anderson—and countless others—are showing us what is possible when we embrace the mission of providing transformational education. In doing so, they have given us more than hope. As New Orleans' influential education reformer Leslie Jacobs told me, "Revolution doesn't happen when things are dismal. Revolution happens on rising expectations." The successful rural and urban educators who are featured in this book—and many others who are not—have started a revolution by showing us what we can expect from our schools.

The history of the United States, from the days of our founding fathers through our civil rights struggles, has been a story of continual quest to live up to our aspiration to be a land of equal opportunity. We can reach this audacious goal. To do so will require that all of us—our political leaders and our civic leaders, our school superintendents and our labor leaders, our teachers and pastors and community leaders, our children and their parents—recognize the stakes for our children and our nation and assume responsibility for the hard work and the change necessary to create a new public education system in our urban and rural communities. Importantly, success will require our future leaders to step up to provide today's children with transformational teaching and to lead transformational change in the future.

If we rise to the challenge, I believe the children in our urban and rural communities will become some of the most inspiring leaders and citizens our nation has ever known—individuals with the fortitude, character, and perspective that come from succeeding in the face of enormous challenges. Like Juan, they will have the skills and motivation to solve other problems, including the challenges of poverty facing their own communities. We can unleash the potential of our urban and rural children to "make history." The question is simply whether we will.

AFTERWORD
Transformational Teaching and Learning Around the World

> There is a universal power in channeling a
> nation's leaders to face its most fundamental challenge.
> —*Alvaro Henzler, cofounder and CEO of EnseñaPerú*

WHEN TARUN CHERUKURI was majoring in chemical engineering at one of India's top engineering colleges, he didn't consider that he might someday soon be teaching in the slums of Pune, a midsize city in the western part of India. Upon graduating, he took a job at Unilever as a technology manager.

In his third year at Unilever, Tarun had the opportunity to volunteer in a school, and what he saw there drew him to an organization called Teach For India when its recruiters led an information session for the young employees at the firm. In a few months, after going through an intensive selection and training program, he was standing before a classroom of thirty-five third grade students in one of the small schools that have cropped up to serve India's neediest students. His third graders showed up in his classroom reading on a kindergarten level and doing math on a beginning first grade level.

Tarun's goal is to get his students on track to college. He has invested his students and their parents in the idea that education is freedom—that it is the path to opportunity—in part through engaging his friends and other community leaders in sharing with the students the stories of their lives. He has built what he calls his "Happy Harvard Classroom," explaining in a welcome to the students and parents that the class is named in this way to bring focus to "our main goals in life and in achievement." His classroom is built around five values—"Happiness is our main goal; Hard work is our only short cut; HUM (which means "we" in Hindi) means we will always be ONE; Honesty is our language; Humility is our dress"—illustrating and reinforcing one of those values each month and eliciting personal reflections on the values from his students' lives every day.

Students track their progress in a way that equates academic progress to the level of universities it prepares them to attend. To put his students on a trajectory to achieve at the highest levels, Tarun brings an intense focus on academics and also finds a way, through spending time with the children outside of the classroom and engaging support from others in his community, to provide them with the extra enrichment of art, music, creative writing, sports, and drama. When he discovered that all his instructional planning and the extra time he spent with his students seemed unlikely to be sufficient for reaching his goal, he enlisted volunteers from his alma mater—eighty of them!—to work with his class.

As I write this book, Tarun is beginning his second year with the same set of students now in fourth grade. He can't yet know whether his work will prove transformational for his students, but he can see that his students have moved from being beginning readers to being able to access encyclopedias and dictionaries on their own. They can manage the classroom in his absence. With most of his students communicating in better English than their seniors at secondary school, their parents have begun to believe that the dream of college can become a reality if their children work hard. For his part, Tarun says, "I strongly believe that my kids will go to college. They already have the intrinsic motivation to make it to the lowest-level colleges. My drive is to get them to believe and rise up to go to the *best* colleges in this country and the world."

Ultimately, Tarun is interested in going into public administration or policy making. He believes a role in these fields will take advantage of his strengths—an ability to work well in analyzing problems and structuring solutions—and of his vantage point from teaching. "Teach For India has made me a convert," Tarun told me. "It has given me a sense of larger purpose towards my nation-building goals."

○ ○ ○

IN ALL THE DISCUSSION about how flat the world is, it has been shocking for me to realize that in India, over a third of students drop out before they complete primary school and the vast majority drop out before completing secondary school.[1] Only a tiny fraction gain access to the kind of education that opens up the full range of professional options to them. What I've learned from social entrepreneurs around the world who have been adapting Teach For America's model in their countries is that the educational inequity that plagues the United States is actually a pervasive global issue. It exists in the most developed countries, even in those whose education systems score well in the international rankings such as Australia, Germany, and the United Kingdom, and in the least developed.

This problem is a threat to human welfare and to the strength of nations around the world, and it is a threat to all of us. In today's world the challenges we face—whether relating to the environment, public safety, disease, or economic welfare—are global in nature. Poverty, ignorance, and lack of education threaten to exacerbate all of our challenges, and improving education is the most promising avenue for tackling them. Increasing educational levels and decreasing educational disadvantage everywhere are key to increasing the well-being of humanity, strengthening governments, increasing tolerance and decreasing terrorism, and generating advances in science, health, and society that will benefit all of us.

○ ○ ○

BEFORE SHAHEEN MISTRI appeared in my office in 2006, I hadn't thought much about whether Teach For America's approach might be applicable in other countries. I knew that Teach First had adapted the model in the United Kingdom, to great effect. Brett Wigdortz launched the first adaptation there in 2002, when he was a management consultant at McKinsey and Company, which had been retained by two business organizations in London to develop a strategy for improving student performance in the city's schools. One of the firm's recommendations was for the launch of Teach First, and with a strong coalition of support among the private sector, the education community, and government, Teach First grew with great success. Today, more than 1,000 participants are teaching across five regions in the U.K., and Teach First is consistently ranked among the country's top ten most prestigious graduate recruiters. The government's inspection system has validated the program's strength and impact through regular evaluations, and the program's alumni, called "ambassadors," have begun assuming leadership roles in education and policy. But despite the success of the model in Britain, I had been so consumed by increasing our impact in the United States that I hadn't given much thought to whether it would be applicable in many other countries.

In India Shaheen had created and grown an organization called Akanksha that ran highly regarded after-school programs in Mumbai and Pune. She was recognized as one of India's most successful social entrepreneurs, and she visited to share her passion for adapting Teach For America's model to India. Although Akanksha had found a way to change students' trajectories through intensive, sustained investment in them, Shaheen was searching for a way to intervene *within* the school day and Teach For India seemed like a way to do this. At the same time, Shaheen recognized that Teach For India could be a source of the leadership necessary to increase the impact of interventions like Akanksha and ultimately to effect fundamental change on a significant scale. She didn't want to reinvent the wheel and was looking for help.

Shaheen is visionary and very persuasive, and so a few months after she appeared in my office I found myself in Mumbai visiting her and others who were interested in creating Teach For India. We visited schools serving children growing up in the city's slums, spoke with potential recruits at college campuses, talked with governmental officials and potential supporters in the private sector, and met with educators and leaders of nonprofit organizations.

In India I was struck by the persistent inequities that are even more significant and more obvious than those in the United States. I was inspired by how energized some of the college students became at the prospect of joining a movement to strengthen India through education, by the enthusiasm among potential supporters in the public and private sectors, and by the need for an additional source of committed, inspired teachers to work with students who were so eagerly waiting for a good education.

As I write this book, Teach For India, which Shaheen launched as an independent nonprofit organization in India, is just placing its second cohort of fellows in schools in Mumbai and Pune and is developing a plan to have 2,000 fellows across ten cities within eight years.

Inspired by Shaheen and by the vision and commitment of several other social entrepreneurs working to adapt the model in their countries, Teach For America and Teach First have worked together to create a global organization called Teach For All, which seeks to expand educational opportunity internationally by increasing and accelerating the impact of this model around the world. Today, three years into Teach For All's history, there are sixteen independent national organizations in the growing network, pursuing a shared mission and theory of change in their countries. Teach For All is working to maximize their scale, impact, and strength through capturing and spreading best practices and fostering connections among the organizations' teachers and alumni so that they can learn from each other across borders.

○ ○ ○

AS MANY DIFFERENCES as there are across the countries represented in Teach For All, I am beginning to see that the causes of the injustice of educational inequity and the solutions may be more similar across countries than not. Tomás Recart, who leads one of the first organizations to join Teach For All, Enseña Chile, recently told me about a meeting he had with several leaders in Santiago—the editor of a prestigious newspaper, business leaders, and other social entrepreneurs—a few days after the results of the yearly educational evaluation were released in Chile: "The results said that again, after twenty years of measurements, there are no significant increases. Year after year, with the publication of these results, all the newspapers are filled by educational experts trying to explain the causes of the problem and the necessary solutions. It is the same thing every year, but no changes occur in our classrooms. The environment of disbelief that every child can learn was present in the air."

Tomás shared a story with the group. He described the transformation of a classroom of one of Enseña Chile's corps members, in a neighborhood so impoverished and dangerous that Tomás had felt compelled to take off his wedding ring as he entered the school. He had seen the teacher change a class of students who weren't paying attention at all and were distracted by their cell phones and their friends into a class of students who were focused on working. She had done this by having a straight conversation with the students about the track they were on and the role education could play in changing that and by empowering them to manage their progress toward clear academic goals. "The students didn't know the stakes—that they'll keep repeating what their parents and grand-parents experienced unless they get a great education," Tomás explained to me. Tomás said that after he shared this story, the people he was meeting with "became silent" and seemed to finally understand. They saw, he said, that success is possible and that the solution is about things we know and can do rather than about politics.

○ ○ ○

IT SEEMS THERE IS MUCH that is universal about education. At the same time, tackling the problem in diverse contexts and cultures will generate powerful new solutions and innovations that can help all of us as we work to ensure educational excellence and equity.

As the Taruns, Shaheens, and Tomáses of the world endeavor to be transformational teachers and leaders, they will generate transformational change in education. Tarun put it this way: "Any sector will thrive and hit a tipping point if a critical mass of the best minds and hearts give their lives to it." Children, families, and nations will benefit. And we will all benefit—because educational levels in any nation impact all of us in today's global world and because there is so much to learn from each other that can benefit our own countries.

I fully anticipate that as we move ahead, leaders around the world will be discovering new answers to educational need and working across borders to accelerate the pace of change for the benefit of society at large. Soon we will have, in dozens of countries around the world, unstoppable movements to realize the day when all children have the opportunity to attain an excellent education.

ACKNOWLEDGMENTS

THE CREDIT FOR ANY POSITIVE CONTRIBUTION this book might make to the quest for educational excellence and equity goes, first and foremost, to the extraordinary Teach For America corps members and alumni and to the educators and partners we are working with in communities across the country. Their love for their students and perseverance on their behalf generated the insights shared in this book.

Teach For America's extraordinary team—our president, Matt Kramer; our leadership team; the executive directors who are leading us forward in communities across the country; and our entire dedicated staff—deserves huge credit for its work in recruiting and developing our growing force of teachers and alumni. The team's deep commitment to our mission and to continuous improvement has been crucial in generating the understanding and the progress this book aims to convey.

While there are so many people who deserve credit and thanks for all their insights and help and feedback, without Steven Farr this book would not have come into existence. His wonderful way with words and his networks throughout the Teach For America community brought these pages to life. And the lessons Steven personally took from his experience as a Teach For America corps member in Texas's Rio Grande Valley and from his years on our staff have measurably deepened the book's substance. We are both grateful to Harley Ungar, our able project manager and thought partner.

I am indebted to Lisa Kaufman, Peter Osnos, and the whole PublicAffairs crew. Their belief in the importance of this book, their patience in the process of getting it written, and Lisa's editing and encouragement have all been vital.

Many thanks to the early readers and constructive critics — Beth Anderson, Monique Ayotte-Hoeltzel, Elisa Villanueva Beard, Catherine Brown, Nick Canning, Elissa Clapp, Aimee Eubanks-Davis, Kevin Huffman, Jason Kloth, Matthew Kramer, and Eric Scroggins — and the many Teach For America staff members and other friends and supporters who have reviewed and contributed to parts of the book.

Finally, I want to thank my husband, Richard Barth, and my kids, for believing in the importance of this work and supporting my professional choices. Their encouragement, perspective, and sense of humor have kept me going.

NOTES

Introduction

1. Teach For America is the most studied teacher education program in the country, and the most rigorous research shows that corps members have a positive impact relative to other new teachers and, in some studies, experienced and traditionally certified teachers in their schools. In 2004 Mathematica Policy Research utilized a gold-standard research methodology—randomly assigning students to the elementary school classrooms of Teach For America corps members and to a control group of other teachers—and found that corps members moved their students forward more than would typically be expected in reading and math; corps members attained greater gains in math and equivalent gains in reading versus students of other teachers, including veteran and certified teachers (Paul T. Decker et al., "The Effects of Teach For America on Students: Findings from a National Evaluation," Mathematica Policy Research, June 2004, http://www.irp.wisc.edu/publications/dps/pdfs/dp128504 .pdf). The education policy journal *Education Next* issued a report card analyzing and grading the most frequently cited studies on Teach For America released before 2008—only the Mathematica study earned an A for its methodology ("Teachers For America: Catalysts for Change or Untrained Temporaries?" *Education Next* 8, no. 2 [2008], http://educationnext.org/ teachers-for-america/). Since then, in 2009, another highly regarded study by the Urban Institute found that in high school, the effect of having a Teach For

America teacher is about twice the effect of having a teacher with three or more years of experience relative to a new teacher (Zeyu Xu et al. "Making a Difference? The Effects of Teach For America in High School," CALDER [National Center for Analysis of Longitudinal Data in Education Research], Urban Institute, 2008–2009, http://www.urban.org/UploadedPDF/411642 _Teach_America.pdf). A 2010 study from the University of North Carolina at Chapel Hill found that corps members did as well or better than traditionally prepared teachers at every grade level and subject level examined; in middle school math, researchers found that corps members added the equivalent of an extra half year of learning (http://publicpolicy.unc.edu/files/Teacher _Portals_Teacher_Preparation_and_Student_Test_Scores_in_North _Carolina_2.pdf).

2. U.S. Department of Education, Institute of Education Sciences, National Center for Education Statistics, National Assessment of Educational Progress (NAEP), 1998, 2000, 2002, 2003, 2005, and 2007 Reading Assessments, http:// nces.ed.gov/nationsreportcard/naepdata/report.aspx.

3. Editorial Projects in Education (*Education Week*), "Diploma Counts," 2009, http://www.edweek.org/ew/articles/2009/06/11/34progress.h28.html.

4. On average, twelfth graders whose family income makes them eligible for free or reduced lunch score at roughly the same level on NAEP reading assessment as eighth graders from wealthier families (National Center for Education Statistics, NAEP, 2005 Reading Assessments, http://nces.ed.gov/ nationsreportcard/naepdata/report.aspx).

5. Bureau of Labor Statistics, December 2009 unemployment data, http:// www.bls.gov/cps/cpsaat7.pdf.

6. Sam Dillon, "Study Finds High Rate of Imprisonment Among Dropouts," *New York Times*, October 8, 2009. See graphic.

7. McKinsey and Company, "The Economic Impact of the Achievement Gap in America's Schools," April 2009, http://www.mckinsey.com/app _media/images/page_images/offices/socialsector/pdf/achievement_gap _report.pdf.

8. James S. Coleman, principal investigator, "Equality of Educational Opportunity Study" (1966), http://www.icpsr.umich.edu/icpsrweb/ICPSR/ studies/06389.

9. "Top New Jersey High Schools, 2008," *New Jersey Monthly*, August 5, 2008, http://njmonthly.com/downloads/1527/download/tophighschools08.pdf.

10. "Education: Westside Story," *Time*, December 26, 1977, http://www .time.com/time/magazine/article/0,9171,919219-1,00.html.

11. Nancy J. Perry, "Saving the Schools: How Business Can Help," *Fortune Magazine*, November 7, 1988, http://money.cnn.com/magazines/fortune/ fortune_archive/1989/12/04/72823/index.htm.

Chapter 1   Teaching as Leadership: Lessons from Transformational Teachers

1. Highland Park Independent School District Web site, http://www
.hpisd.org/Default.aspx?tabid=53.

2. http://www10.ade.az.gov/ReportCard/SchoolReportCard.aspx?id=878
83&Year=2008&ReportLevel=1.

Chapter 2   No Shortcuts: Lessons from Transformational Schools

1. For the definition of "exemplary" in the context of Houston schools, see
http://ritter.tea.state.tx.us/perfreport/account/2010/manual/table6.pdf.

2. Christopher B. Swanson, "High School Graduation in Texas: Independent
Research to Understand and Combat the Graduation Crisis," Editorial Projects in Education Research Center, October 2006, http://www.edweek
.org/media/texas_eperc.pdf.

3. YES College Preparatory Schools business plan (in possession of the author).

4. Eighty percent of high-income, college-qualified high school graduates from
the class of 2004 are projected to earn a bachelor's degree by 2012 ("Mortgaging
Our Future: How Financial Barriers to College Undercut America's Global Com-
petitiveness," a Report of the Advisory Committee on Student Financial Assistance, September 2006, http://www2.ed.gov/about/bdscomm/list/acsfa/mof.pdf).

5. Gary Scharrer, "Report Points to Dropout Factory," Houston Chronicle,
November 7, 2007.

6. Christina Clark Tuttle et al., "Student Characteristics and Achievement
in 22 KIPP Middle Schools," Mathematica Policy Research, June 2010.

7. Joshua D. Angrist et al., Who Benefits from KIPP? (Cambridge, MA:
National Bureau of Economic Research, May 2010), http://www.nber.org/
dynarski/w15740.pdf.

8. New York City develops an annual progress report for each school in
the district. A school's overall score is a weighted average of scores along four
dimensions: school environment (based on parent and teacher surveys and
other data about attendance, communication, engagement, safety, respect,
and so on), accounting for 15 percent of the score; student performance
(in English and math), accounting for 25 percent; student progress (average
student improvement from prior year in English and math), accounting for
60 percent; and additional credit provided for closing the achievement gap
contributing up to another 15 percent. In 2007–2008 KIPP Infinity scored
97.7, which placed it in the number-two position overall and the number-one
position for elementary and middle schools. In 2006–2007 KIPP Infinity
scored number two overall and for elementary and middle schools. As of
2008–2009 KIPP Infinity still ranks in the top 10 percent overall in elementary

and middle schools (NYC Department of Education, 2009–2010 Progress Reports for Schools, http://schools.nyc.gov/Accountability/tools/report/default.htm).

9. *2003 Community Health Report: Denver Harbor/Port Houston Super Neighborhood* (Houston: St. Luke's Episcopal Health Charities, April 2003), http://www.slehc.org/HNI/HNI_Reports/upload/DH_PH_Community %20Profile.PDF.

10. Mastery Charter School Web site, http://www.masterycharter.org.

11. Ibid.

Chapter 3   Scaling Success: Lessons from Improving Systems

1. Web site of the New York City Department of Education: http://schools .nyc.gov.

2. Hedrick Smith, "Making Schools Work," interview with Joel Klein, http://www.pbs.org/makingschoolswork/dwr/ny/klein.html.

3. New York City Department of Education, http://schools.nyc.gov/Accountability/data/TestResults/NAEPReports/default.htm.

4. Charles Sahm, "NYC Reforms Still Working," *New York Post*, August 13, 2010.

5. New York City Department of Education, "NYC Graduation Rates Class of 2009 (2005 Cohort)," March 2010, http://schools.nyc.gov/Account ability/Reports/Data/Graduation/GRAD_RATES_2009_HIGHLIGHTS.pdf.

6. Dorothy Givens Terry, "Staying Afloat in New Orleans," November 7, 2007, http://diverseeducation.com/article/10283/.

7. "KIPP New Orleans Schools Strategic Business Plan, 2009–10 and Beyond" (in possession of the author).

8. Sarah Laskow, "Necessity Is the Mother of Invention," *Newsweek*, August 26, 2010.

9. Education Trust, "Yes We Can: Telling Truths and Dispelling Myths About Race and Education in America," September 2006, 8.

10. National Assessment of Educational Progress, National Center for Education Statistics (U.S. Department of Education), 2007, http://nces.ed.gov/nationsreportcard/naepdata.

11. D.C. Public Schools Facts and Statistics Web site, http://www.dc .gov/DCPS/About+DCPS/Who+We+Are/Facts+and+Statistics.

12. National Assessment of Educational Progress, National Center for Education Statistics (U.S. Department of Education), 2007, http://nces.ed.gov/nationsreportcard/naepdata.

13. "Graduation Rate Trends, 1996–2006," *Diplomas Count, 2009* (published by *Education Week*) 28, no. 34 (2009).

14. U.S. Department of Education, "Revenues and Expenditures for Public Elementary and Secondary School Districts: School Year 2006–2007 (Fiscal Year 2007)," http://nces.ed.gov/pubs2009/2009338.pdf.

15. Michelle Rhee commentary in *Forbes Magazine*, January 23, 2008.

16. "The Nation's Report Card, Mathematics 2009: Trial Urban District Assessment," http://nces.ed.gov/nationsreportcard/pubs/dst2009/2010452 .asp.

17. DCPS press release, July 13, 2010, http://dcps.dc.gov/DCPS/In+ the+Classroom/How+Students+Are+Assessed/Assessments/DCPS+ Secondary+School+Students+Demonstrate+Significant+Gains+for+Third +Consecutive+Year.

18. DCPS press release, October 5, 2010. Also, Census of Enrollment of the District of Columbia Public Schools and Public Charter Schools, the District of Columbia State Education Office. Report from October 5, 2009. http://seo.dc.gov/seo/cwp/view,a,1222,q,552345,seoNav,%7C31195%7C.asp.

19. Louisiana's Race to the Top Application, Appendix A3: Growth in Recovery School, http://www.louisianaschools.net/lde/r2t/.

20. Educate Now! analysis of the spring 2010 test results of the Louisiana Educational Assessment Program (LEAP), http://educatenow.net/2010/ 05/26/analysis-of-the-spring-2010-test-results/.

21. Brian Thevenot, "Paul Pastorek Ruffles Feathers as State School Superintendent," *New Orleans Times-Picayune*, August 2, 2009.

22. Paul Tough, "A Teachable Moment: Education in a Post-Katrina New Orleans," *New York Times Magazine*, August 17, 2008.

23. Testimony to the U.S. Government Accountability Office, "District of Columbia Public Schools: While Early Reform Efforts Tackle Critical Management Issues, a District-Wide Strategic Education Plan Would Help Guide Long-Term Efforts," Statement of Cornelia M. Ashby, Director of Education, Workforce, and Income Security. March 14, 2008, http://www.gao.gov/ new.items/d08549t.pdf.

24. June Kronholz, "D.C.'s Braveheart," *Education Next* 10, no. 1 (2010), http://educationnext.org/d-c-s-braveheart/.

25. "Schools to Lack Books, Repairs as Classes Resume," *Washington Times*, July 31, 2007, http://www.washingtontimes.com/news/2007/jul/31/schools -to-lack-books-repairs-as-classes-resume/.

26. DC Appleseed and Piper Rudnick, "A Time for Action: The Need to Repair the System for Resolving Special Education Disputes in the District of Columbia," September 2003.

27. Kronholz, "D.C.'s Braveheart."

28. V. Dion Haynes, "Parents Protest Plans for School Closures," *The Washington Post*, February 28, 2008.

29. Bill Turque, "New D.C. Ratings Stress Better Test Scores," *Washington Post*, October 1, 2009.

30. The New Teacher Project Web site, http://www.tntp.org/index.php/our-impact/highlights/new-orleans/.

31. New Leaders for New Schools Web site, http://www.nlns.org/Locations_NewOrleans.jsp#results.

32. Lucia Graves, "The Evolution of Teach For America," *U.S. News and World Report*, October 17, 2008.

Chapter 4   Silver Bullets and Silver Scapegoats

1. Pennsylvania Department of Education, "2008–2009 PSSA and AYP Results," http://www.portal.state.pa.us/portal/server.pt/community/school_assessments/7442.

2. KIPP Gaston College Preparatory Web site, http://kippgaston.org/.

3. U.S. Department of Education, National Center for Education Statistics, "2009 Digest of Education Statistics," table 182, http://nces.ed.gov/programs/digest/d09/tables/dt09_182.asp.

4. NAEP data from "The Nation's Report Card: Trends in Academic Progress in Reading and Mathematics, 2008," http://nces.ed.gov/nationsreportcard/pubs/main2008/2009479.asp. SAT data from College Board SAT, "2007 College-Bound Seniors: Total Group Profile Report," 2007, http://www.collegeboard.com/prod_downloads/about/news_info/cbsenior/yr2007/national-report.pdf.

5. This refers to the dollars in cumulative spending per student per point on PISA (the OECD's Programme for International Student Assessment) in mathematics, 2004. McKinsey and Company, "The Economic Impact of the Achievement Gap in America's Schools," April 2009. McKinsey analysis based on OECD 2006, http://www.mckinsey.com/app_media/images/page_images/offices/socialsector/pdf/achievement_gap_report.pdf.

6. Census of Enrollment of the District of Columbia Public Schools and Public Charter Schools, the District of Columbia State Education Office. Report from October 5, 2007. http://seo.dc.gov/seo/frames.asp?doc=/seo/lib/seo/information/school_enrollment/2007-2008_Final_Audit_Report.pdf.

7. Center for Education Reform, Annual Survey of America's Charter Schools, January 2010, http://www.edreform.com/Resources/Publications/?Annual_Survey_of_Americas_Charter_Schools_2010.

8. Stanford University, Center for Research on Education Outcomes (CREDO), "Multiple Choice: Charter School Performance in 16 States," June 2009, http://credo.stanford.edu/reports/MULTIPLE_CHOICE_CREDO.pdf.

9. Patrick J. Wolf, "The Comprehensive Longitudinal Evaluation of the Milwaukee Parental Choice Program: Summary of Third Year Reports," SCDP Milwaukee Evaluation, Report #14, April 2010, http://www.uark.edu/ua/der/SCDP/Milwaukee_Eval/Report_14.pdf.

10. Patrick Wolf et al., "Evaluation of the DC Opportunity Scholarship Program, Final Report," National Center for Educational Evaluation and Regional Assistance, U.S. Department of Education, June 2010, http://ies.ed.gov/ncee/pubs/20104018/pdf/20104018.pdf.

11. Jay P. Greene and Marcus A. Winters, Manhattan Institute for Policy Research, "When Schools Compete: The Effects of Vouchers on Florida Public School Achievement," August 2003, http://www.manhattan-institute.org/html/ewp_02.htm.

12. Bill and Melinda Gates Foundation, "All Students Ready for College, Career, and Life: Reflections on the Foundation's Education Investments, 2000–2008," http://www.gatesfoundation.org/learning/Documents/reflections-foundations-education-investments.pdf.

13. "Evaluation of the Bill and Melinda Gates Foundation's High School Initiative, 2001–2005 Final Report," prepared by The American Institutes for Research and SRI International, August 2006, http://www.gatesfoundation.org/learning/Documents/Year4EvaluationAIRSRI.pdf.

14. Bill Gates, speech to the Forum on Education, November 11, 2008, http://www.gatesfoundation.org/speeches-commentary/Pages/bill-gates-2008-education-forum-speech.aspx.

15. U.S. Department of Education, http://www2.ed.gov/programs/teacherqual/2010findings.doc.

16. "The State of Tennessee's Student/Teacher Achievement Ratio (STAR) Project: Final Summary Report, 1985–1990," http://www.heros-inc.org/summary.pdf.

17. CSR Research Consortium, "What We Have Learned About Class Size

Reduction in California," September 2002, http://www.classize.org/tech report/CSRYear4_final.pdf. In 1996 the California legislature passed SB 1777, a reform measure aimed at cutting class size in the early school grades from what had been an average of twenty-nine students to a maximum of twenty.

18. In "Don't Forget Curriculum," an August 2010 Brookings Institution paper by Grover J. "Russ" Whitehurst, the author argues that the "effect size" of curriculum exceeds that of any other education reform analyzed (http://www.brookings.edu/papers/2009/1014_curriculum_whitehurst.aspx).

19. Interview with Steve Jobs, April 20, 1995, Smithsonian Institution Oral and Video Histories, http://americanhistory.si.edu/collections/comphist/sj1.html.

20. William L. Sanders and June C. Rivers, University of Tennessee Value-Added Research and Assessment Center, "Cumulative and Residual Effects of Teachers on Future Student Academic Achievement," November 1996, http://www.mccsc.edu/~curriculum/cumulative%20and%20residual%20effects%20of%20teachers.pdf.

21. Erik Hanushek, "The Single Salary Schedule and Other Issues of Teacher Pay," October 2006, http://edpro.stanford.edu/hanushek/admin/pages/files/uploads/Teacher_incentives_salaries.pdf.

22. Bill Gates, speech to the American Federation of Teachers, July 10, 2010, http://www.aft.org/pdfs/press/sp_gates071010.pdf.

23. Robert Gordon, Thomas J. Kane, and Douglas O. Staiger for the Hamilton Project, *Identifying Teacher Effects Using Performance on the Job* (Washington, DC: Brookings Institution, April 2006), http://www.brookings.edu/views/papers/200604hamilton_1.pdf.

24. Ibid.

25. Howard S. Bloom, Saskia Levy Thompson, and Rebecca Unterman with Corinne Herlihy and Collin F. Payne, "Transforming the High School Experience: How New York City's New Small Schools Are Boosting Student Achievement and Graduation Rates," MDRC, June 2010, http://www.mdrc.org/publications/560/overview.html.

26. Mathematica Policy Research, "An Evaluation of Teachers Trained Through Different Routes to Certification," report prepared for the Institute of Education Sciences, February 2009, http://ies.ed.gov/ncee/pubs/20094043/pdf/20094043.pdf.

27. See Evan Thomas and Pat Wingert, "Why We Must Fire Bad Teachers,"

Newsweek, March 6, 2010, http://www.newsweek.com/2010/03/05/why-we -must-fire-bad-teachers.html; and Daniel Weisberg et al., the New Teacher Project, *The Widget Effect: Our National Failure to Acknowledge and Act on Differences in Teacher Effectiveness*, 2009, http://widgeteffect.org/down loads/TheWidgetEffect.pdf.

28. Trip Gabriel, "Despite Push, Success at Charter Schools Is Mixed," *New York Times*, May 1, 2010.

Chapter 5   Increasing the Pace of Change

1. Weisberg et al., the New Teacher Project, *Widget Effect* (see chap. 4, n. 26).

2. NYC Teaching Fellows Web site, https://www.nycteachingfellows .org/about/program_statistics.asp; and NYC Teaching Fellows Media Kit, http://www.nycteachingfellows.org/mypersonalinfo/downloads/PressKit_ WE_2010.pdf.

3. U.S. Census Bureau, *2009 Statistical Abstract*, "Table 246: Public Elementary and Secondary School Teachers-Selected Characteristics," http://www .census.gov/compendia/statab/cats/education.html.

4. Donald Boyd et al., Urban Institute, "The Narrowing Gap in New York City Teacher Qualifications and Its Implications for Student Achievement in High Poverty Schools," September 2007, http://www.caldercenter .org/PDF/1001103_Narrowing_Gap.pdf.

5. Jim Collins, *Good to Great: Why Some Companies Make the Leap . . . and Others Don't* (New York: HarperBusiness, 2001), 13, 1. See also Ed Michaels, Hellen Handfield-Jones, and Beth Axelrod, *The War for Talent* (Boston: Harvard Business School Press, 2001).

6. Richard Ingersoll and Lisa Merrill, "Who's Teaching Our Children?" *Educational Leadership*, May 2010, http://www.ascd.org/publications/ educational-leadership/may10/vol67/num08/Who's-Teaching-Our -Children%C2%A2.aspx.

7. Arthur Levine, Education Schools Project, "Educating School Teachers," 2007, http://www.edschools.org/pdf/Educating_Teachers_Report.pdf.

8. The 340 most selective public and private colleges are from *U.S. News and World Report's Best Colleges*, http://colleges.usnews.rankingsandreviews .com/best-colleges. The percentage of graduates from these schools who are African American, Latino, and from low-income backgrounds is found in U.S. Department of Education, National Center for Education Statistics

(2007–2008 data), "Integrated Post Secondary Education Data System," http://nces.ed.gov/ipeds/datacenter/.

9. Kevin Carey, "Hot Air: How States Inflate Their Educational Progress Under NCLB," *Education Sector* (May 2006).

10. Michael Johnston and Christine Scanlan, "Clarifying Colorado's Teacher Bill," *Denver Post*, May 23, 2010, http://www.denverpost.com/opinion/ci_15129751?source=bb.

11. "Tenure Bills Nears Passage," *Denver Post*, May 12, 2010, http://www.denverpost.com/education/ci_15066164?source=pkg.

12. Richard Lamm, Roy Romer, Bill Owens, and Bill Ritter, "Great Education System Requires Great Teachers, Principals," *The Colorado Springs Gazette*, April 24, 2010.

13. Dawn Ruth, "Leslie Jacobs," *New Orleans Magazine*, December 2008, http://www.myneworleans.com/New-Orleans-Magazine/December-2008/Leslie-Jacobs/.

Chapter 6   Transformational Teaching as the Foundation for Transformational Change

1. Dan Cray, "Elementary Schools of the Year: Like a Free Private Academy," *Time*, May 21, 2001, http://www.time.com/time/magazine/article/0,9171,999915,00.html.

2. Donna Foote, "Lessons from Locke," *Newsweek*, August 11, 2008, writing about her book *Relentless Pursuit: A Year in the Trenches with Teach For America* (New York: Alfred A. Knopf, 2008).

3. Green Dot press release, August 16, 2010, http://www.greendot.org.

4. The Watts–Beverly Hills API gap was calculated by using the average API of all schools in the respective districts for the years 2000 and 2009. In 2000 the API gap was 422; by 2009 it had been reduced to 232 (Academic Index Reports on the California Department of Education Web site, http://dq.cde.ca.gov/dataquest/).

5. America's Promise Alliance, "Cities in Crisis, 2009: Closing the Graduation Gap," http://www.americaspromise.org/~/media/Files/Resources/CiC09.ashx, 15.

Afterword   Transformational Teaching and Learning Around
             the World

1. According to the World Bank EdStats Web site, the drop-out rate at the primary level in India is 34.2 percent (original source: UNESCO Institute for Statistics in EdStats, October 2009, http://web.worldbank.org/WBSITE/ EXTERNAL/TOPICS/EXTEDUCATION/EXTDATASTATISTICS/EXT EDSTATS/0,,menuPK:3232818~pagePK:64168427~piPK:64168435~the SitePK:3232764,00.html). According to a report prepared by India's Department of Higher Education, India's Gross Enrollment Ratio for secondary and higher secondary schools is 39.91 percent (http://www.ibe.unesco.org/ National_Reports/ICE_2008/india_NR08.pdf).

Wendy Kopp is the founder and chief executive of Teach For America, the cofounder and chief executive of Teach For All, and the author of *One Day, All Children*. She lives in New York City.

Steven Farr, Teach For America's chief knowledge officer, is the author of *Teaching As Leadership*.

PublicAffairs is a publishing house founded in 1997. It is a tribute to the standards, values, and flair of three persons who have served as mentors to countless reporters, writers, editors, and book people of all kinds, including me.

I. F. STONE, proprietor of *I. F. Stone's Weekly*, combined a commitment to the First Amendment with entrepreneurial zeal and reporting skill and became one of the great independent journalists in American history. At the age of eighty, Izzy published *The Trial of Socrates*, which was a national bestseller. He wrote the book after he taught himself ancient Greek.

BENJAMIN C. BRADLEE was for nearly thirty years the charismatic editorial leader of *The Washington Post*. It was Ben who gave the *Post* the range and courage to pursue such historic issues as Watergate. He supported his reporters with a tenacity that made them fearless and it is no accident that so many became authors of influential, best-selling books.

ROBERT L. BERNSTEIN, the chief executive of Random House for more than a quarter century, guided one of the nation's premier publishing houses. Bob was personally responsible for many books of political dissent and argument that challenged tyranny around the globe. He is also the founder and longtime chair of Human Rights Watch, one of the most respected human rights organizations in the world.

· · ·

For fifty years, the banner of Public Affairs Press was carried by its owner Morris B. Schnapper, who published Gandhi, Nasser, Toynbee, Truman, and about 1,500 other authors. In 1983, Schnapper was described by *The Washington Post* as "a redoubtable gadfly." His legacy will endure in the books to come.

Peter Osnos, *Founder and Editor-at-Large*